King Jo**H**n

Lady Gl**A**nusk

Howel Gw**Y**nn

Ri**C**hard Booth

Willi**A**m de Broase

Matilda de **S**t Valery

William La**T**ham Bevan

Co**L**onel Morrell

Richard W**E**llington

Peter Ford retired to live in mid-Wales. He developed a keen interest in local history and became a town guide. His passion is to tell the often-forgotten stories of local people. To explore the lives of those who may have been forgotten, or who suffered misfortune. Folktales abound in rural locations. Where do they come from and how much truth is there in them?

Also by Peter Ford.

Matilda – Lady of Hay.
Logaston Books.

Mary Morgan of Presteigne.
Victim or Villain of 18th Century Infanticide.

Fair Rosamund.
Mistress to King Henry II.

Doctors, Disease and Death.
The Story of Public Health in Hay on Wye.

Weston.
The Often Forgotten Suburb of Hay on Wye.

Available from Amazon.

HAY CASTLE MANSION

A SOCIAL HISTORY

1122 – 2022

PETER FORD

Amazon Paperback.
Copyright © Peter Charles Ford.
First published in Great Britain in 2022.
Peter Charles Ford has asserted his right to be asserted as the author
of this work in accordance with the
Copyright, Design and Patents Act 1988.

All rights reserved.
No part of this publication may be reproduced, stored in a retrieval system,
or transmitted, in any form or by any means
without the prior written permission of the publisher,
nor be otherwise circulated in any form of binding or cover
other than that in which it is published
and without a similar condition being imposed on any subsequent purchaser.

To Angela.
Your help and support made this book possible.

Acknowledgements.
Tim Pugh, with Eric and June, kindly allowed me access to the 'Pugh Archives' for information
and images related to Old Hay and its inhabitants.

Hay Castle Mansion and front lawn pre-1939 viewed from the south.
The keep and great gates are to the right.
From a postcard published by H.R. Grant, Stationer, Hay.

Introduction

This is the story of some of those who breathed life into the fine old building known for centuries as Hay Castle. Most of the original castle is long gone but we have basic details about the occupiers. There is much more information about the families who lived in the Jacobean mansion built in 1640 on the castle site.

Sometimes the occupiers were the owners and the lords of the manor. At other times the owners of the castle were not the lords of Hay. For many years it was rented to tenants.

In many instances the owners did not live at the castle, or even anywhere near Hay. Particularly in the early days, Hay was just another estate and lordship they held and not an important one at that. Later they may have been absentee landlords, but they liked the prestige of giving Hay Castle as their address.

Tenants may have been relatives of the lords, particularly during the 19th and 20th centuries. Regardless there was always a constant stream of notable guests who visited and often stayed there.

Inevitably information about this motley collection of people is patchy. While details may be sparse in the early years more information starts to come to light as the centuries pass. This is particularly so during the last two hundred years.

Only the shell of the keep, the magnificent gateway, and a fragment of the medieval walls remain of the ancient castle. For a detailed history of the medieval structure, readers are referred to Paul Remfroy's 'Hay Castle'.

The history of the lordships of Hay, and these were the lords who usually owned the castle, is covered by Alan Nicholls in 'The Lords of Hay'.

By convention, the mansion has always been referred to as 'Hay Castle' or Hay Castle Mansion although it ceased to be a castle nearly 500 years ago.

Contents

Introduction vi
List of Illustrations. 8
Chapter 1 – Hay Castle in the March. 9
Chapter 2 - Jacobean Mansion. 25
Chapter 3 - Hay Vicarage 45
Chapter 4 - The Golden Age - People 67
Chapter 5 - The Golden Age - Events 85
Chapter 6 – Fire! Fire!. 99
Chapter 7 - Hay Castle Trust. 113
References 115

List of Illustrations.

Hay Castle Mansion and front lawn pre-1939 viewed from the south......................v
Wales at the time of the Norman conquest...10
Clifford Castle..12
Motte and bailey castle shown in the Bayeux tapestry...14
The north town side of the castle...15
Statue of dog and Norman head that guarded the keep for 800 years.......................16
Effigy of Moll Walbee..19
Plan of the castle site...26
Detail of the Boyle mansion..27
Fragments of Venetian glass..28
Town of Hay...30
Musket powder measure..32
Hay drawn by Robert Batty...35
Memorial to Richard Wellington...37
Hay in 1741 by Henry Gastineau...39
Glass bottle seal of R Wellington...41
The Nantyglo ironworks Monmouthshire...48
Sales by Auction...49
Coach house...51
The Keep by George Woods 1816..52
Rev. William Latham Bevan..53
Rev. W.L. Bevan with his family 1895...55
The archdeacon on his jubilee...62
Diocesan History St David's..64
Meet of Hounds, Town Clock, Hay..68
Hay Castle Fish and Game book...77/8
John Jones head gardener and Mrs Madigan..81
Parents of 'Boys at the Front' 1915..86
Midshipman Hon. B.M. Bailey HMS Defence...89
Maypole dancing on the front lawns...91
George Psalmanazar native of Formosa..94
Ancient key to the castle..98
Butchers shop of William Keylock pre-First World War..100
Bill for Hay Fire Brigade for the 1939 fire..102
Richard Booth – Coeur de Libre..106
The upper floor of the mansion after the 1977 fire...108
The puzzling lintel on the first floor..110
Public domain images are subject to the Creative Commons license https://creativecommons.org/publicdomain/zero/1.0/ and the Creative Commons Attribution-ShareAlike 2.0 license. https://commons.wikimedia.org/wiki/Creative_Commons.

Chapter 1 – Hay Castle in the March.

In the early days of the Norman conquest of Wales **Hay Castle** was a minor power base protecting the Wye corridor from Hereford to Brecon. It was built by Bernard de Neufmarche to provide security to the rich arable lands of the county of Herefordshire. It acted as a deterrent to those in Wales who periodically conducted border raids, as well as provided protection to the growing population of **Hay** and the surrounding countryside.

The town's location was the key to its role. **Hay** sits in the valley of the Wye at the confluence of the counties of Radnorshire, Breconshire, and Herefordshire.

To the south and west are the uplands of the Brecon Beacons and the Black Mountains, and to the north are Radnor Forest and Cambrian Hills. This was border country, with the indigent Welsh population occupying the uplands while the invading Normans preferred the richer agricultural lowlands.

In medieval times the valley of the Wye was the major southern gateway from England into Wales. It was less risky than travelling the northern route through Chester, dominated as it was by the Welsh stronghold of Snowdonia.

The Wye Valley led to the ancient Welsh kingdom of Brycheiniog, centred on modern-day Brecon. From there the southern and western March, and southern Snowdonia, were easily accessible.

To understand the early inhabitants of the castle and who held the power in the area it is necessary to understand the role of the castle and its place in the March.

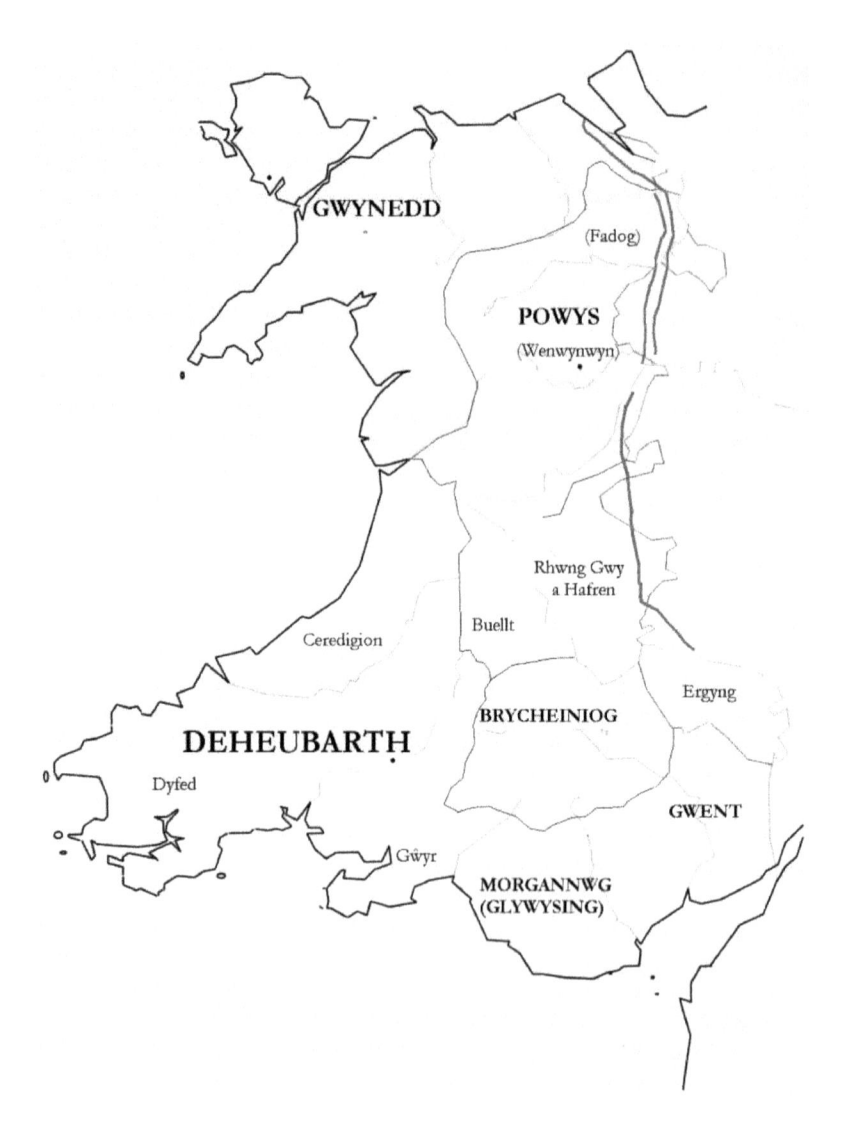

Wales at the time of the Norman Conquest.
Hay lies in the northeast corner of what was known as Brycheiniog.
This work has been released into the public domain by its author **Owj20**.

The March.

When William the Conqueror defeated Harold at the Battle of Hastings that was just the start of the conquest of his new kingdom. It took him eight busy years to subdue the country as far north as Northumberland.

On his journey there he came to the Welsh-English border but did not have the time, or resources, to advance further westwards. He took one look at the harsh and bleak Welsh countryside, consisting of hills and valleys, bogs and forests, with little useful agricultural land, and decided he would not go there.

From his standpoint, the Welsh population was sparse and scattered, with no major centres of population to conquer. There was little prospect of drawing the Welsh into a pitched battle. He did not have the time for a guerrilla war, armed as the Welsh were with their special version of the longbow. This was made from a dwarf elm tree. The arrows did not travel as far as the English longbow but it was very powerful over shorter distances and the ideal weapon for forest ambush.

William's strategy was to create the earldoms of Chester, Shrewsbury, and Hereford. He appointed three of his most loyal, trusted, and fearsome knights to them with instructions to establish their control over the Welsh-English borderlands. This area is what became known as the Welsh March or Marchia Walliae.

To keep out insurgents they were permitted to invade Wales to put down rebellions and impose their authority. To do this they were given rights by the monarch, such as raising their own armies, waging war against the Welsh or fellow lords in the March, and building castles as required. All this was without specific royal permission, an unusually high degree of semi-independence from the control of the monarch.

A characteristic of William the Conqueror, noted by an English monk in the Anglo-Saxon Chronicle, was common to all Normans.

Into avarice did he fall
And loved greediness above all.

By this he meant greed for gold. With gold soldiers could be hired and that meant security, and security meant power. In the March the same philosophy was applied to land. If Normans held the land they could travel easily to control any rebellious Welsh uprising and then assert their authority by building castles at strategic strongpoints.

The Founding of Hay.

The origins of '**The Hay**' are obscure. Before the conquest this was part of an area called Haeg by the Anglo-Saxons, meaning a clearing in land used for hunting. Post conquest it was given the name Haiae meaning a wooded area with clearings within it surrounded by a fence or hedge, again used as a deer park. An area such as this was the private domain of the king or a senior lord.

Despite the existence of a ford across the Wye, and the subsequent passage of persons of note, very few people would have been living adjacent to it. Living in a deer park was not allowed, and a ford meant an army could pass. Regardless of whether this was Norman or Welsh, plundering for food, or worse, was always a possibility. In addition, farming would have been easier on the flat farmland east of the Dulas Brook in Herefordshire or west of the Loggin Brook on the Welsh side of the town, although this did not preclude the odd peasant scratching a living in the area.

Clifford Castle dominated the Wye Valley between Hereford and Hay.

It was the first earl of Hereford, William Fitz Osbern, who started the southern Norman incursions into Wales when he defeated the three Welsh kings of Brycheiniog in 1070. To protect his route along the Wye valley and deter Welsh incursion into England, he built a castle at Clifford three miles to the east on the Hereford side of **Hay**.

William died in 1071 while fighting in Flanders and his son Roger of Breteuil became the second earl. An early undated charter exists which may relate to him. This granted the church of St Mary in Clifford 'free license to buy or sell without toll or other restraint in **Hay**, Brecon and all his tenements near the Wye'. A Church of St John is mentioned *c*.1144 but whether this was the forerunner of the chantry chapel in **Hay** dedicated to the saint is unknown.

This indicates there was already a settlement in the area although there was no mention of **Hay** in the Doomsday Book of 1086. It is believed that this was because it is in Wales, unlike Clifford which is in England. Roger was unseated after a short time following his support for the Revolt of the Eagles against William the Conqueror. Bernard de Neufmarche was appointed in his stead.

Bernard was an obscure Norman knight who appears not to have held any lands in England before the Doomsday Book. William gave him lands in Herefordshire and the Golden Valley, essentially along the river Wye. This may have encouraged him because very shortly after 1086 he advanced into Wales along the valley from his castle at Clifford.

After passing a ford crossing the river adjacent to a small settlement (Hay?) he advanced as far as Glasbury by 1088 and Brecon by 1093. Bernard killed Rhys ap Tewdwr King of Deheubarth and Bleddyn ap Maenarch King of Brecheiniog at the battle of Cwmgwernygad. Brecon then became his Welsh base and he immediately started to build a castle above the rivers Usk and Honddu and founded a priory on the spot where Rhys had been killed.

To protect his access to Brecon, and reward the 15 knights who had accompanied him, Bernard divided his new territory, including along the Wye Valley, into manors and gave it to them[1].

They owed allegiance to Bernard but followed his example and built their own strong points. In this way they dominated the area and ensured that Norman access to Brecon was protected.

Initially the local centre of habitation was not in Hay by the ford but half a mile west where a small stream called the Loggin Brook tumbled down from the hills into the river. Here a fortified strongpoint, a motte and bailey castle, was built around 1090. This area was a separate legal entity from the town of Hay and was known as Weston Hamlett until the 1600s.

Eventually, 30-40 years later, a castle had been built to the east on the high bluff overlooking the ford. This was well established by 1155 when houses within it were granted to Brecon Priory. The castle dominated the centre of the town which grew up below it and was later enclosed by town walls. It became known as **'The Hay'**, a name that endured for centuries.

Motte and Bailey Castles.

The motte and bailey castle was William the Conqueror's 'secret weapon' in his conquest of his new kingdom. They were quick and easy to build and provided a secure strong point from which to dominate and control the local countryside.

A motte and bailey castle is shown in the Bayeux Tapestry.
Public domain under the creative commons licence.

All the castle consisted of was a large mound of earth, the motte, with a wooded defensive tower on top. Surrounding it was the bailey, a palisade or wooded fence enclosing storerooms, stables, barracks, smithy, and kitchens. All the resources of labour and materials needed to build it were readily available locally, particularly if there was a handy hill nearby which could be utilised.

Many were rudimentary affairs, especially if placed on a hilltop, while others were more elaborate with very large mottes and very deep surrounding ditches. The English-Welsh border is still dotted with the remains of numerous mottes, indicating just how many must have been built. Nationally the remains of almost 1,000 have been identified.

By their very nature they were temporary structures. Prone to rot or burning, some failed to be occupied, and others fell out of use within twenty or so years. As the Normans consolidated their hold more secure stone-built castles either replaced them or were erected on better defensive sites with deeper ditches and steeper sides or stronger walls.

Hay Castle.

The original castle in the **Hay** area, 'Castello de haia' as it was called by Henry I, was a motte and bailey built by Sir Philip Walwyn near St Mary's Church in the area called Weston. It was created around 1080 -1100 but probably occupied for less than 50 years. All that has survived is the earth mound, now known as the Tump. Until the mid-1600s legally it lay outside the town of **Hay,** the area of which was defined by the town walls eventually built by Eva de Braose.[2]

Later a second castle was built. Its founding is unclear. It was recorded that Bernard de Neufmarche built a castle in **Hay** around 1121, a few years before he died. Possibly this was another motte and bailey on the bluff in the centre of town although it may have been the square stone tower on the same site now referred to as the keep.

Whichever it was, and it might have been that both were built within a few years of each other, the bluff soon developed into a strong military structure.

The north town side of the castle pre-1939 showing the keep and great gates.
From a postcard published by Thomas Moxon of Hay.

Originally the stone tower was a gatehouse with large doors in the front and back giving access to the bailey, a wooden fenced enclosure around the top of the bluff. This rapidly superseded the motte and bailey built down near the church and became the major stronghold in the area.

Despite the Norman incursions into Wales the Welsh constantly pushed them back. For two centuries they continued to periodically attack the castles at Radnor and Painscastle, a few miles north of **Hay** in Radnorshire. This meant that **Hay Castle**, dominating the other side of the Wye on the border of Breconshire and Herefordshire, was important as a Norman frontier fortress.

In practice this situation did not persist for long. As the Normans pushed back the Welsh, despite their odd major incursions, the castles at Brecon and Builth became the main frontier fortresses.

Hay remained a relatively small, fortified site. A new entrance with large gates was added around 1200-1240 and later strengthen with a portcullis. These superseded the original gates in the tower which were blocked up to create a strong point, and what became known as the keep.

Stone walls were built to replace the wooden palisade surrounding the site. A great hall and chapel were added later. Documents mention another gatehouse and drawbridge, and these were probably built on the opposite side of the site from the keep.

A statue believed to be of a dog was found during the recent renovations.

The Norman head that guarded the keep for 800 years.

The early history of the castle.

Hay Castle passed through multiple hands over the next 400 years. Whether any of the owners lived in it, with one notable exception, is unlikely but possible. It is more probable that they might stay a night or two as they passed to and from Wales. Their bailiffs were more likely to be the principal occupants, appointed to collect the lord's taxes.

- Bernard de Neufmarche died around 1123-25. His wife Nest (Agnes) FitzRichard was the daughter of the Welsh princess Nest, daughter of Gruffydd ap Llywelyn and Edith of Mercia. Bernard had a son Mahel but because he mutilated the paramour of his widowed mother, she denounced him as illegitimate. He was disinherited and Henry I arranged for Bernard's daughter Sybil to marry one of his strongest supporters Miles of Gloucester. By doing so Miles acquired the lands of Bernard which included **Hay Castle**. All four of Mile's sons died relatively young and without heirs so Mile's daughter Bertha inherited her father's estates.

- Bertha had married William II de Braose, lord of Bramber, sometime before 1150 so when her last brother died in 1166 **Hay Castle** passed through her to become one of the de Braose estates. The early history of the castle is inextricably linked to the de Braose family. William I de Braose arrived in England with the Conqueror in 1066. Since then successive generations of the family had acquired lands in Bramber, Barnstaple, Totnes, Radnor and Builth, and now the lordships of Brecon and Abergavenny, as well as **Hay**.

- When William II died sometime between 1180-90 his son William III inherited. Earlier he nearly caused the downfall of the family. William III lost favour with Henry II after the notorious incident of the massacre of Abergavenny. On Christmas Day 1176 he invited Seisyll ap Dinfnwal and other Welsh princes with their entourages to a banquet at Abergavenny Castle. He persuaded them to leave their arms outside when they went in to dine in the great hall. William then locked the doors, and his men went in and killed all 75 of them. Seisyll's seven-year-old son Cadwallader was pursued and killed, allegedly by William's hand. For this incident, he became known as 'the ogre of Abergavenny'.

- For the next 20 years little is heard about the family until William III became a prominent supporter of King Richard the Lionheart in the 1190s and accompanied him campaigning in France. From about 1200 William became the most important baron in the country after helping to put King John on the throne. William also fought extensively with him in France as well as conquered much of South Wales. **Hay** was one of his holdings and he and his wife Matilda de St-Valery were key players in the early history of the area. **Hay Castle** was Matilda's powerbase and Brecon Castle was Williams.

Matilda Lady of Hay.

The most famous occupant of the castle, certainly in medieval times, was Matilda de St-Valery. William granted some of his lands to his wife and **Hay** was part of them. She based herself here in mid-life, after bringing 16 children into the world.

She was a formidable woman and **Hay** became not only her source of revenue but from where she protected and supported her husband's Welsh 'empire'. Allegedly she led her own army into Elfael (southern Radnorshire) while her husband was fighting in Brecon and Builth.

In 1198 Matilda was at the fortified ancient hill fort of Painscastle four miles north of **Hay** when it was attached by the Welsh prince Gwywynwyn. Matilda held the besieging army off with her few followers for three weeks until the English raised an army to lift the siege, killing 3,000 Welshmen in the process. It was said that the river Bachwy ran red with their blood, and a nearby prehistoric burial mound was referred to as their mass grave for years.

Matilda was in control of the area when Archbishop Baldwin of Canterbury, with Giraldus Cambrensis (Gerald of Wales), passed through Wales recruiting for the Third Crusade. On 7 March 1198, Ash Wednesday, Giraldus gave a sermon at **Hay Castle**, and the archbishop stayed the night.

There are strong circumstantial indications that around 1200 Matilda took key responsibility for building and/or extending the castle. This included constructing a new stone perimeter wall and a new gateway, now known as the Great Gates. She also blocked up the arches in the old gatehouse tower. This may have been a direct result of her experience at Painscastle and the realisation that the existing defences at **Hay** were inadequate.

Subsequently numerous legends grew up about her, particularly among the Welsh. She 'built' **Hay Castle** in a night and as she was carrying the stones in her apron one fell into her clog. In anger she picked it up and threw it across the Wye to the village of Llowes three miles away. It now resides in the church as St. Maelogs Cross; one of the finest Celtic slab crosses in Wales.

It may be that Matilda had the new walls of her castle lime washed so that they suddenly appeared on the horizon, giving the impression that they were built in a night. She may also have arranged for the Celtic cross to be placed in Llowes churchyard to mark the grave of the hermit of Llowes. He was an interpreter of dreams for the famous cleric Gerald Cambrensis – Gerald of Wales.

These legends may relate somehow to the Welsh tradition of the Ty Uunos or 'House in a Night'. If someone could build a house in a night on common ground, and have a fire in the hearth by morning, they could claim squatter's rights and the house was theirs. In addition, by throwing an axe (the stone cross?) from each corner the resultant area became the garden of the house.

Matilda was hated by the Welsh who called her Moll Walbee – the Welsh witch.

This effigy in St Mary's Church Hay is traditionally said to be 'Moll Walbee'. Photograph by the author.

The de Braose Downfall.

The downfall of the most powerful baron in the land was sudden and dramatic. It stemmed from King John's demand for the 40,000 marks that he claimed William III owed him. This was an enormous sum and to secure the debt King John suggested his heir, William IV, came to court. In effect, he would become a hostage until his father paid the money.

There is a widespread belief that Matilda was in **Hay** when the king's messenger asked for her son and grandson. Matilda refused to release them because she said King John could not be trusted. This stemmed from the uncertainty over what happened to Prince Arthur of Britany.

Henry II had four sons. The first Young Henry predeceased him, so Richard the Lionheart became king. On his death Henry's third son Geoffrey would have inherited but he had predeceased Richard. Under current law Geoffrey's son Prince Arthur of Brittany would have inherited the crown. Unfortunately for him at that time inheritance was less certain. Arthur was 12 years old, only spoke French, and had never been to England. That did not help his claim. William III managed to convince the other barons that they would be better off with Henry II's fourth, youngest, son Prince John however vain and untrustworthy he was.

Subsequently Arthur disappeared. Later William III claimed to have witnessed King John murder Arthur in a drunken rage in Rouen at Easter 1202. This was not general knowledge at the time. William made this accusation after he was in exile in France, but he may have told his wife confidentially shortly after the incident. By mentioning it Matilda let the secret out and incurred the wrath of King John.[1]

In not handing over family hostages, and making comments about Arthur, Matilda had effectively sealed the fate of the de Braose family. They were outlawed. King John gathered an army and pursued them to Ireland. Initially, Matilda and her children managed to escape to Scotland but were soon captured. Matilda and her eldest son, William IV, were taken to Corfe Castle and starved to death by King John. William III managed to flee to France where he died a pauper.

Matilda is known as The Lady of Hay. It was King John who called her Maud de la Haie, or **Matilda Lady of Hay**, during her lifetime.

For a fully detailed account of her life, death, and the legends, of this (most) important occupier of the castle in Medieval times see:

Matilda – Lady of Hay, by Peter Ford.
Logaston Books, (2021).

Aftermath.

When the de Braose family was outlawed by King John he put one of his mercenaries in control of their lands, but it was not long before **Hay** passed in and out of de Braose family control again.

- At the outlawing **Hay** was granted to Gerald d'Athee, the sheriff of Gloucester. Shortly afterwards he was superseded by Engelard Cigogne. Matilda's sons Giles and Reginald then wrestled **Hay** back from Engelard. This provoked King John, and he came to **Hay** from 27-29 July 1216 to burn and plunder the town and destroyed the castle.[2] Giles died soon after.

- Two years later King Henry III succeeded to the throne and came to **Hay** where he confirmed Reginald as holder of the de Braose lands. Reginald was succeeded by his son, William V who married Eva Marshal, daughter of the great William Marshall, and they lived at **Hay Castle**.

William V was captured by Llywelyn ap Griffith and had to agree to the marriage of his eldest daughter, Isabelle, to Dafydd the son of Llywelyn. William V had no male heir which meant in time Dafydd would inherit **Hay**. At Easter 1230 Llywelyn discovered a liaison between William V and his wife, Joan, the illegitimate daughter of King John. On 2 May Llywelyn hanged William V at Crokin, then destroyed **Hay Castle**. Despite this, the arranged marriage between Isabelle and Dafydd went ahead. The Welsh language play Siwan (Joan) is based on these events.

- Despite Dafydd effectively inheriting **Hay Castle** there followed a period of confusion. King Henry III took the de Braose estates, including **Hay** and gave them to various parties including William Marshal, Hubert de Burgh, and 'finally' Earl Richard of Cornwall, the king's brother. Walter de Godardville was the custodian of the castle in July 1231 when King Henry III returned with his army to organise the rebuilding of 'Maud Castle' at Painscastle. It may be that **Hay Castle** had a dry moat at this time[3]. Henry Turbeville of Crickhowell was appointed the new custodian.

- The following year Eva de Braose, wife of William V who had been hanged by Llywelyn, was handed the castle by Henry Turbeville on King Henry III's instructions. Henry also gave her 12 marks and permission to raise a murage tax every week for three years. With this, she built the town walls around **Hay**. Shortly afterwards Eva died and the king granted Brecknock including **Hay** to Earl Humphrey Bohun for his son, and his wife Eleanor de Braose. This was the time, 1252, when the protracted disputes over the de Braose lands were finally agreed upon.

a) Matilda de Braose (wife of Roger Mortimer of Wigmore) took Radnor and Presteigne.
b) Eve de Braose (wife of William III de Cantaloupe) took Abergavenny.
c) Eleanor de Braose (wife of Humphrey de Bohun V) received Brecknock, including Hay. The de Braose family rose to dominate the Welsh heartlands and hold Hay through William III, but in the following generation their power was lost. A generation later their name had all but disappeared from the March.[4]

Swansong of the Castle.

As estates and castles passed to more and more powerful men the periods of their occupation or even visits, became less and less. These were volatile times, and the lords were constantly changing. The affairs of court, from Edward I-V, Henry III-VIII and Richards II and III, were more important than those of a minor castle in an obscure corner of Wales. The following lords of **Hay** owned the castle but as far as is known never resided there.

- Humphrey V de Bohun inherited **Hay** through his wife Eleanor de Braose. At the battle of Cefnllys in 1262 most of the Norman gains of 200 years were lost and he was left with just Brecon and **Hay**. King Henry III then transferred these to Roger Mortimer, as heir of William de Braose.

- On 11 July 1264 **Hay Castle**, under Roger Mortimer's constable William Hackelutel, surrendered to Simon de Montfort. Simon moved on to his demise on 4 August at the battle of Evesham four weeks later. **Hay** was then passed back to the Bohuns but unfortunately at the battle Humphrey Bohun V had been badly injured and died a short while afterwards.

  The Inquisition on his death (effectively the probate record) revealed the revenue of the lordship of Hay was £122 3s 4d. This was made up of:

Demise lands	£16 0s 0d.
Town rents and tolls	£22 0s 0d.
Rent of the town oven	£6 13s 4d.
The fishery	18s 0d.
Passagium – protection of the highway	£1 12s 0d.
Foreign rents – from outside parish	£6 13s 4d.
Cowyield – 22 cows and calves per year	£3 12s 4d.
Pannage of swine	10s 0d.
Customary Welsh works	£7 17s 8d.
Mills	£15 0s 0d.
The Prise of ale	£13 12s 4d.
Meadows	£6 13s 4d.
Pleas and perquisites of Court	£22 0s 0d.
Garden with fishpond and dovecot	10s 0d.

- Custody then becomes very confusing. Humphrey V's father Earl Humphrey IV Bohun took over, with Hugh de Dynneton as his constable. Humphrey IV died on 24 September 1275 and his grandson Humphrey VI then inherited, but he was still a minor.

- By now Roger Mortimer had re-established himself at **Hay Castle** but he was mandated by the king to deliver the castle to (his rival) Gilbert Clare, during the minority of Humphrey VI. Roger was later granted £217.5s.8d in compensation. When Humphrey VI reached 18 years he was confirmed as heir to the castle and town of **Hay**. He died aged 50 and was succeeded by his son.

- Humphrey VII Bohun married Elizabeth, the widowed daughter of King Edward I. Humphrey and a number of barons rebelled against Edward II due to his favouritism of the two Hugh Despenser's, father and son, who were despised by many. The rebellion ended with their defeat at the Battle of Boroughbridge on 17 March 1322. Hugh Despenser was then granted lands taken from the rebellious barons including **Hay**. Robert Morley probably became the temporary keeper of **Hay** and Brecon Castles. John Gardyner was the bailiff in 1372.

- Humphrey X Bohun inherited the castle early in 1373 but he died almost immediately leaving two daughters, Eleanor and Mary, both minors. **Hay** was taken into Crown Trusteeship.
    a) Eleanor married first, to Thomas of Woodstock, son of Edward III, in November 1376. As Mary was still a minor Thomas was able to claim her inheritance of **Hay**.
    b) Mary married Henry Bolingbroke, the future Henry IV, and he then claimed **Hay** although this was only a life interest.

- Mary and Henry's son King Henry V came to the throne on 20 March 1413, and he passed **Hay** to the Earls of Stafford through Eleanor and Thomas' daughter Ann in 1444.

Dukes of Buckingham (Earls of Stafford).

Humphrey Stafford, 6th Earl of Stafford, (15.08.1402-10.07.1460) was made the 1st Duke of Buckingham in 1444, and **Hay** was one of his estates. This was a time of general anarchy with the country occupied with the Wars of the Roses and political upheaval. He is unlikely to have even noticed let alone visited this obscure corner of the kingdom. Following his rebellion, Humphrey was killed at the Battle of Northampton on 10 July 1460. At his post-mortem **Hay Castle** was said to be ruinous, destroyed by the Welsh.

Humphrey's grandson Henry Stafford (4.09.1455-2.11.1483) became the 2nd duke. He helped put Richard III on the throne in 1483 but was executed by him for rebellion when he supported Henry Tudor's claim to the throne. Two years later his son Edward Stafford became the 3rd Duke. He was executed by Henry VIII on 17 May 1521 after claiming descent from Edward III and foolishly indicating a desire to succeed to the throne. The title then fell into abeyance.

Despite most of Buckingham's lands being forfeit to the crown Edward's son Henry Lord Stafford (1501-1563) was eventually given a small part of them including **Hay**. This passed to Henry the 2nd Baron Stafford, but he died soon after on 1 January 1566. His younger brother, another Edward (17.01.1536-18.10.1603), became the 3rd Baron Stafford. During his lifetime, sometime after 1589, **Hay** passed to James Boyle Sheriff of Hereford.

During the times of the Dukes of Buckingham and Lords Stafford, approximately 1440 to 1590s, the castle slumbered on with no real importance either militarily or administratively. The country was occupied with the Hundred Years War, the Wars of the Roses, the Black Death, and the rise of the Tudor court.

Oblivious to the power politics at court, who owned the castle was of academic interest to the locals. They were more concerned about the bailiff appointed to look after it. He was a very important person. Everyone paid their taxes to him and protested any injustices through the leet court he presided over. An example was hearing a number of inquisitions at the castle during 1278-9 into the litigation that followed Llywelyn's defeat and withdrawal from the March.

The three waves of the Black Death in 1348-50, 1361-62 & 1369 killed around one-third of the three million population of the country. It appears **Hay** escaped the first two waves very well. Not the third, and the nearby hamlet of Wern Wood ceased to exist. In 1298, before the Black Death, the population of the town has been estimated to have been 550 people.

In 1298 **Hay Castle** was valued at 6 shillings per annum, and in 1362 the castle with appurtenants was £50. Rental income between 1371-98 was approximately £115 p.a. In the 1380s the porter received 8d per week as wages with a yearly allowance of 6s.8d. for expenses. At around this time, Richard Mogholom the bailiff made a claim for an iron chain and lock to help secure the lord's boat/ferry on the river Wye. This possibly crossed the river at Steeple Pool near the church.

Owain Glyndwr.

Despite a long-held belief that Glyndwr destroyed **Hay Castle** around 1403, Fairs[5] concluded that he did not. This has been endorsed by more recent thinking that suggests Glyndwr bypassed it. Perhaps he thought it was 'sufficiently Welsh' not to attack it, or perhaps his army was too weak after the sweating sickness that ravaged his troops at the siege of Caernarvon.

In practice, it was the threat from the rebellion that led to the castle being put into good repair in the years from around 1400. To improve the defences £24.3s.8d. was spent on the 'great tower' i.e. the keep, and £82.18s.8d. on the building of a new chapel and chamber.

The rebellion also created a fear of a future attack, and so in 1404 the castle was stocked with 20 quarters of wheat, 80 quarters of oats, 450 fish, 8 tuns of ale and 2 tuns of wine. The garrison was also increased from 16 to 88 men-at-arms and 80 to 220 archers. We do not know how long this extra vigilance lasted but it must have persisted for a time because continual repairs were done each year between 1410 and 1416 to the gateway, drawbridge, tower, and internal buildings. At this time 20 archers were sent from the castle – 'Hays Land'- to the battle of Agincourt in 1415.

Despite the strengthening works between 1400 and 1416 when John Leland visited **Hay** on his itinerary in 1538 he stated that:

> *'Ther is also a castel, the which sumtime hath bene right stately'.*[6]

Regardless of the odd prestigious visitor, **Hay** town slumbered peacefully on fully occupied in the daily tasks of trying to earn a living.

Chapter 2 - Jacobean Mansion.

The exact configuration of the medieval castle is unknown, although we know it had the key features of gates, a keep, a great hall, and a chapel, as well as a drawbridge and moat. Most of these have been swept away but it has continued to be described as 'the castle' despite it being principally a mansion house from *c*1640.

There are features in the Jacobean mansion that may be remnants of the original castle.

- A wall to the left-hand side of the great hall in the east wing as you enter from the front gardens is eight feet thick. This separated the hall and the more public reception area from the private family quarters, where the present café is situated. It was unnecessarily thick for the newly built structure.

- A second wall at the extreme left-hand side of the main mansion, now at the far end of the café, is fifteen feet thick and may have been the end wall of the great hall. The enormous fireplace is not in the middle of this wall suggesting the room was originally larger. The 'cut out' damage on the left-hand side of the fireplace is due to a small Victorian fireplace fitted in the middle of this wall when the room was reduced in size and the fireplace boarded over.

It is assumed that as these walls are over-generous for the mansion they represent the incorporation of the remaining features after the castle ceased to be militarily significant.

With the unification of the Principality under the Council of Wales in 1535 peace descended on the March. After the formal union of England and Wales in 1542 the Welsh and English were no longer fighting each other, militarily at least, so the castles along the border became redundant. Their continued use depended more on their suitability as administrative centres than on their use as living accommodation.

Hay Castle had always been too small to provide spacious living accommodation and by this time was in a general state of disrepair. Nevertheless, it was the most important building in an important market town that sat at the junction of the three counties of Herefordshire, Breconshire and Radnorshire.

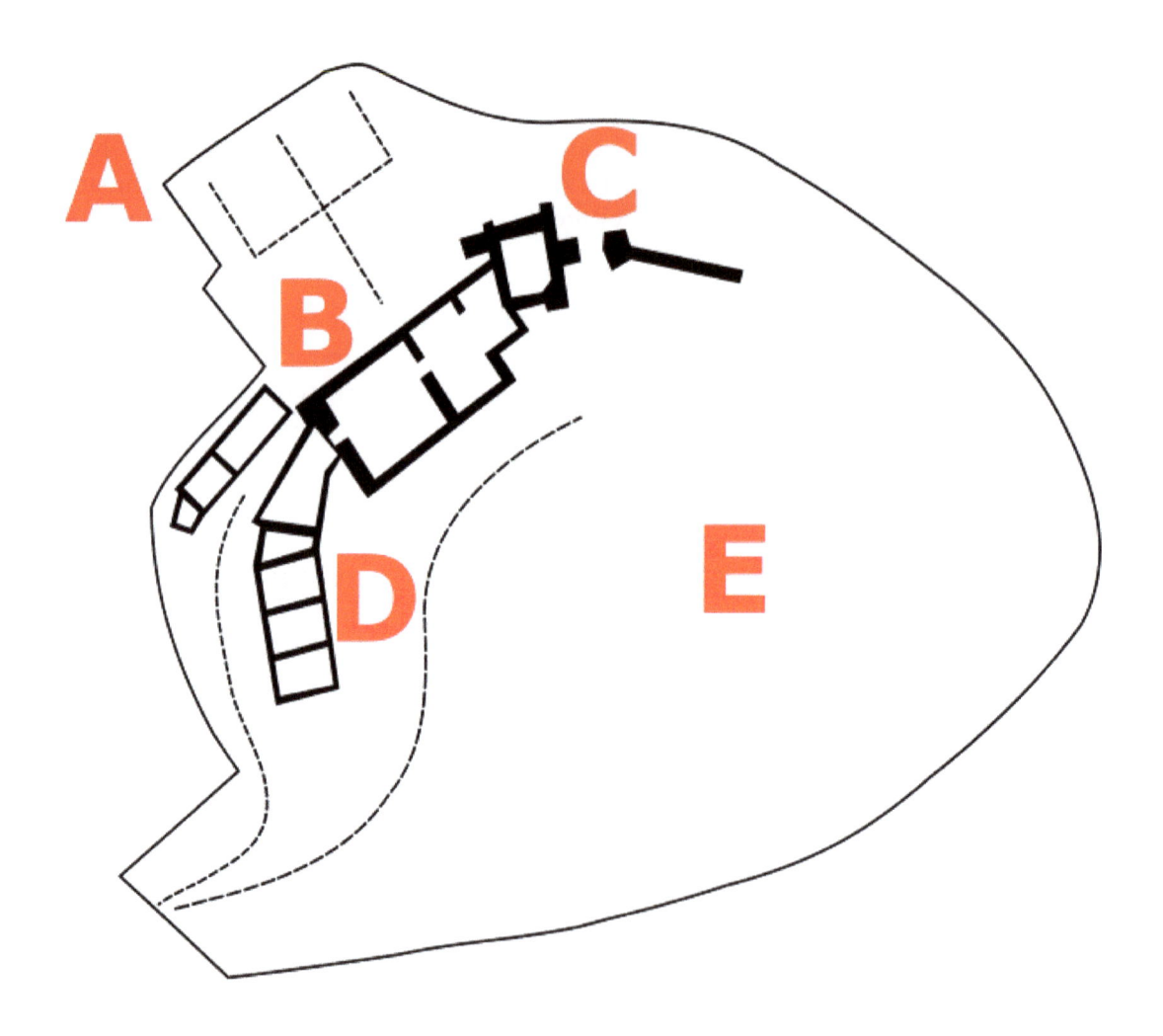

Plan of the castle site in the 21st century.
A – terraced gardens; B – mansion; C – keep and gateway;
D – stable and service block; E – rear garden.
This file is licensed under the Creative Commons Attribution-Share Alike 4.0 International license.

James Boyle.

Before he died in 1547 Henry VIII created James Boyle, born *c*1530 in Dilwyn Herefordshire, sheriff and mayor of Hereford. Elizabeth I must have approved the appointment as he was still in post in 1588, the year of the Spanish Armada, and one year after Elizabeth had executed her half-sister Mary Queen of Scots.

Amongst the estates associated with the Hereford mayoral role in 1544 was the land of Greyfriars Priory. James managed to attach the manor of Hay to it, 'by some irregular means'. Regardless of how he did so, he became the lord of Hay and he put a new building on the Hay Castle site. Whether for himself or members of his family we do not know.

The castle had been militarily unimportance for the previous 150 years and was virtually derelict. The previous lord's bailiffs may have lived there but the owners had not done so, consequently, there was no one to ensure its upkeep.

The narrow wall of the small Boyle mansion abutting the medieval keep. Note the low window showing that the original ground level was raised later.

The rebuilt north wall of the keep overlooking the town. This shows the new fireplaces, new windows, and a stairwell within the wall.

James's new building was small but by abutting it up to the medieval keep he was able to incorporate that into his mansion. He cut new doors through the walls, so the inside became a usable space. The north wall overlooking Castle Square was rebuilt entirely with new windows and two new fireplaces. The wooden lintels are still in place and dendrology shows that they date to c1575 so giving us an approximate timescale for James' new development. New spiral stairwells passing from floor to floor within the walls were also incorporated at that time.

Recent archaeology has demonstrated that the new half of his mansion was built over the foundations of the curtain wall. We do not know to what extent he demolished the Great Hall or the chapel, but as they were reportedly derelict the stone would have provided a useful source of building material.

Fragments of Venetian glass were recently found in the area of the keep.

Fragments of two drinking vessels were recently found in this area. One was a goblet with a white enamel cross and foliate design under a band of stylised cable on a colourless glass base. This dates from the mid-16th century.

The other was a Venetian style, *façon de Venise*, bellied tankard. Its manufacturing technique involved coating a clear base layer with another layer of glass incorporating threads of white glass. This type of decoration dates from the mid-16th century. Together with shards of window glass, these fragments reflect the high status of James Boyle's mansion.[9]

As the lord of the manor, James was entitled to the tolls from the markets and traders. He acquired a bad reputation for his unlawful collection of them, for which he was fined on more than one occasion.[10] James also hired out the market hall for his own benefit although the inhabitants of the town had built it for their use.

His bailiffs were noted for their aggressive approach to their work. There were frequent complaints of assault on market holders, and one stated in his will that he was ill and died because of villainy by William Smythe the bailiff of Hay.

In this aggressive approach, James was no worse than many other lords who employed bailiffs to 'strong arm' their tenants. As the castle was technically outside the town it was outside the jurisdiction of the ancient baronial court and was said to have formed a sanctuary for debtors.

James married Ann Lewis of Hampton Court (near Leominster) and had three sons and something like eight daughters. His eldest son James married Catherine, daughter of Watkins Vaughan of Bredwardine. Catherine remarried in 1584 to Sir Henry Coates of Semer in Suffolk so James must have been deceased by then. Catherine seems to have been unlucky in her choice of husband as after Sir Henry she married Robert Whyte of Aldershot.

James and Catherine's eldest son, another James, had two daughters Anne, who married James Tomkyns of Monington and Weobley, and Mary who married Howell Gwyn IV of Trecastle in the early 1590s. The two girls were co-heirs so on their father's death Mary's share passed into the wealthy Gwyn family.[11] They then purchased Anne's share.

Howell Gwyn maintained his estate at Trecastle when he was made High Sherriff of Brecknockshire in 1603 and 1615.[12] It was through his son Thomas that the Gwyn family created a significant presence in Hay.

Panoramic View of Hay from Mouse Castle

The town of Hay nestling in the Wye Valley.
The castle lies in the jumble of roofs seen in the middle of the picture.
From a postcard published by H.R. Grant, Stationer, Hay.

Thomas Gwynn.

Thomas Gwynn (note the multiple alternative spellings of the Gwyn surname) of Hay, a member of the local gentry, was a colonel in the Royalist army in the civil war. Upon his surrender he is reputed to have cried 'Hey God. Hey devil. I will be for the stronger side.' Being on the losing side does not appear to have harmed Thomas' career.

Thomas married Catherine Ann the daughter of Walter Vaughan of Merthyr-Cynog.[13] Thomas is credited with building the present Jacobean Mansion House on the castle site, dated by dendrology to 1636. The size and style of his grand mansion testify to his wealth and status. Thomas incorporated the new build section of the Boyle mansion into his new property but excluded the medieval keep element of it.

One local historian has always suspected that 'the mansion was built on the site of the great hall, lord's chamber, and other 'high-status rooms' of the former castle'.[14] What is certain is that after the building of the Boyle mansion, and before the Gwynn mansion was started, the ground level of the castle site on which the mansion now sits was raised by approximately six feet (1.8m) of topsoil.

This increased elevation made the new mansion more imposing from the town side but may have removed any trace of a gateway, moat or bridge on the Oxford Road side of the site. This amount of earth moving was a phenomenal undertaking before modern earth-moving equipment. Where could all the earth have come from?

- One speculation is that it may have been spoil from the building of the terraces and landscaping on the town side of the mansion. This side of the castle must have had a gentler slope up to the great gates at one time if horses were able to haul wagons up and through it into the castle bailey.

- Alternatively, or in addition, it may have been from a large motte in the middle of the front lawn, all that was left from Bernard de Neufmarche's original Hay castle. Flattening this would have opened up the view of the Black Mountains to the south.

- Another possibility is that the bluff the castle was built on was uneven, and levelling or flattened of a small hillock or undulation on top was desirable. It needs further excavation to see the extent of the medieval surface covered by the full six feet of soil to help clarify this.

Regardless of where the soil came from the effect was to elevate the mansion and so allow it to further dominate the town. The town side became the back as Thomas made his front entrance off Oxford (also known as Horsefair) Road.

During Thomas' time there were further complaints about the tolls at the two weekly markets and three annual fairs. Nationally the lords of manors continued to be very unpopular for the setting as well as the collection of tolls and were often prosecuted for abuses. Hay featured in a number of legal tussles including one at the Court of the Star Chamber.[15]

Theophilus Jones in his History of the County of Brecknock, Glanusk ed. observes 'Mr Gwyn and his brother in law …. are stated … to have imprisoned several persons and to have extorted large sums by way of toll from those who came here to fairs and markets, but upon their appearance and disclaimer … the trifling crimes of false imprisonment and exhortation (were) forgotten and forgiven.'

In 1629 the Gwynne family rescinded their claim to Welsh Hay and were consequently granted the manor of English Hay. Perhaps it was just coincidental that this was the year Thomas was made High Sheriff of Brecknockshire. He described himself as being 'of Hay Castle'.

Thomas Gwynne died in 1644 leaving the mansion to his son Howell. Sadly Howell only lived for a further five years before dying on 26 June 1649. This meant that Thomas' main beneficiary became his second son, David. Thomas's wife Thomazine continued to describe herself as 'of the Hay Castle' so she continued to live there until she died in 1658.

Despite the same name, Thomas was not the father of the celebrated Hereford beauty, and mistress of Charles II, Nell Gwynne. He was also called Thomas but only achieved the rank of captain in the Royalist army (1642-51). He retired to become a brewer.

A post-medieval musket powder measure, probably dating to the English civil war, found in the castle grounds.

Gwynne Inheritance.

David Gwynne died in February 1652 with no issue. He left no will and the mansion and estate, valued at £500, then reverted to his sisters, the four daughters of Thomas - Ann, Elizabeth, Rachel and Mary. Each of them inherited one quarter in accordance with Welsh inheritance laws.

- Ann married Walter Vaughan of Trebarried (d.1697) son of Roger Vaughan of Clyro. Trebarried was one of the most important estates in the county of Breconshire at this time.
- Elizabeth never married and left her quarter portion of the castle to her sister Ann.
- Rachel had no children and left her portion to her husband Richard Gwynn of Gwempa. He ran into financial difficulties and sold his quarter part in 1721 to pay debts.
- Mary did not have any children either. She died before 1697 and her husband Edward Williams does not figure in the later history of the mansion. On that basis, Mary may have passed her share to one of her sisters, or Edward may have sold it back to the family.

The four sisters were described as dividing the mansion into separate apartments. The configuration of these is not known but we can speculate. One apartment could have used the existing stairs of the main Jacobean stairwell in the great hall, a second the servant's stairs in the middle of the house and a third the back stairs into the servant's block.

Was it coincidental that around this time a new fourth stairwell was installed? At the top of the flight of steps leading up from the present Honesty Bookshop lawn in Castle Street, there is a door opening into the building (the present bookshop). Originally this was a small entrance hall. In creating the fourth apartment the door was sealed, the hall ceiling cut back, and a new staircase was inserted. The window above it was enlarged to light the new stairs, and the adjacent ground-floor window into the hall was modified to become a new door. (The stairwell was destroyed in the fire of 1977. In the redevelopment this doorway was reopened).

The effect of this change was to turn the mansion into a terrace of four units.[16] It is not clear how many of the four part-owners lived in the mansion. It is quite possible the married sisters lived at their husband's properties and let their portions out, although Elizabeth certainly lived there.

In 1682, during the sister's time in the castle, Henry Somerset was created the Duke of Beaufort by Charles II. He was appointed the Lord President of the Council of Wales and Lord Warden of the Marches and made a grand tour of the March in 1684. During the tour he made a 'semi-royal' visit to Hay on 5 August 1684 and was 'handsomely entertained' in the castle by Elizabeth.[17] It seems likely that Ann and Walter would not have missed this golden opportunity to be there, and possibly Rachel and Richard and Mary and Edward, but there is no record to substantiate that any of the other sisters were also in attendance.

In recent archaeological excavations fragments of two glass domestic dishes were found in the keep tower, one more robust than the other, and both show heavy signs of wear. They may relate to this time and suggest a normal domestic environment rather than the high-status tableware of James Boyle's time.[18]

Elizabeth was held in high esteem in the town. She died on 12 May 1702 and was buried on the south side of the altar[19] in St. Mary's Church, Hay. The large grave slab to the Gwynns was relocated in the church rebuild of 1834 and is mounted inside the church on the west wall.

> HERE WERE INTERRED THE
> BODIES OF THOMAS GWYNN
> OF Y HAY CASTLE ESQ. HOW
> EIL GWYNN HIS SON AND HEIR
> AND Y VERTUOUS AND MOST
> CHARITABLE VIRGIN. ELIZA
> BETH GWYNN DAUGHTER AND
> COHEIRE OF Y SAID THOMAS
> GWYNN. SHE FOUNDED AN
> ALMES-HOUSE IN THE HAY
> FOR SIX POOR PEOPLE AND
> ENDOWED IT WITH AN AN
> NUAL GIFT TOWARDS THEIR
> RELIEFE FOR EVER. SHE DE
> PARTED THIS LIFE THE 12TH
> DAY OF MAY ANO: DME:
> 1702

In her will, Elizabeth endowed 'a habitation for six of the most poor, weak and indigent people of Hay'. Her original building was in Chain Alley on Ship Pitch, but it became derelict. In 1876 it was rebuilt in St Mary's Road and continues to offer almshouse accommodation.[20]

Hay Castle was described as sold to the Wellington family in 1721 by the Gwynnes after they introduced a private Act of Parliament. Despite this, it seems the Gwynn family remained part owners as over 100 years later they were a party in the sale of Hay Castle to Joseph Bailey in 1844.

At this time the lordship separated from the ownership of the site. It went from Walter Vaughan to his brother Gwynn and then to his daughter the Hon. Roach Vaughan who described herself as 'of Hay Castle'. Roach married the Hon. Rev. John Harley and so the lordship passed into the Harley family, the earls of Oxford. (For further information please refer to The Lords of Hay by Alan Nicholls.)

HAY.

Hay.[21] The mansion is clearly depicted dominating the skyline.
Drawn by Robert Batty, d. 1848 and engraved by Edward Francis Finden, 1791-1857.
Public domain.

The Wellington Family.

The first identified member of the Wellington family in the area was John who lived at the Priory, Clifford. The Wellingtons were an important family of mercers and publicans and John owned extensive land at Kington, Brilley and Clifford as well as multiple inns in Hay.

When he died in 1708 it was his son Richard who succeeded him and started the direct Wellington family connection with the castle. This lasted for around 100 years. Like many families, they tended to use the same forenames from generation to generation. In the Wellington's case it was Richard and Henry, and these names occurred regularly in siblings' families as well. This makes following the lines of succession complicated to unravel and for this I am indebted to The Lords of Hay by Alan J. Nicholls.

Richard I Wellington (1674-8.9.1732).

Richard lived at the Wellington family home, the Priory, Clifford but he also owned at least two houses in Hay as well as multiple farms in west Herefordshire. In 1721 he bought Hay Castle (or at least part of it as discussed) when the Gwynne family sold it to pay off debts.

Richard continued to live at Clifford all his life although when he was made High Sheriff of Brecknockshire in 1726 he gave his address as Hay Castle. This was despite selling 'the castle, messuage, capital mansion house, together with outhouses, courts, yards, gardens, and orchards,' all known as Hay Castle, to his son Richard II for the sum of 5s in 1725. Later evidence seems to suggest he only sold part of the property as the Gwynn family retained an interest.

The sale also involved multiple other properties and land. These are difficult to identify after all this time because property descriptions tended to refer to the former or current tenants rather than their street address.

In Hay, the land included the two fields Kae Mawr and Kae Bach at the southern end of the present car park leased to Edward Wellington Richard I's youngest brother, and two seats on the south side of St Mary's Church 'between the chancel and the reading pew'.[22] There was other land as far away as Glasbury and Gwynyfed.

In 1725 Richard married his second wife Anne Smyth. They had a daughter Anne in 1726 and a son George in 1731. The following year Richard died. He left a very detailed will covering outstanding loans, debts, crops and agricultural items, as well as household goods.

Richard had a younger brother Edward who had a son, another Edward. He was an apothecary and sometimes referred to as a surgeon. Although born locally he worked in St Paul's Covent Garden where he acquired a considerable fortune. In addition to land at Gravesend he owned a number of holdings in Hay, Brecon and Hereford.

The memorial to Richard I Wellington d.1732. Originally inside the building it was moved outside to the north wall of St Mary's church after the rebuild in 1834.

Richard's second wife Anne was his executor. She was soon in dispute with the children of Richard's first wife Mary over the administration of his will, and provision for her and her children. The conflict revolved around whether she was his servant at the time of their marriage. Anne denied she was, although admitted she lived with him 'as his housekeeper' before marriage.

Richard's estate at Clifford passed to his daughter, and son-in-law James Woodhouse. Later the Priory appears in the wills of Richard's descendants so this may have only been a life interest. Richard's daughter Mary married Walter Watkins of Llydiady Wain, Cusop. Their son Walter received £5000 Consolidated Bank Annuities in a prenuptial settlement in 1743 when he married Myra Taylor of Birmingham.

Richard II Wellington (1698-29.6.1760).

Richard II was the son of Richard I and his first wife Mary. He married his cousin Dorothy (1701-12.12.1765), daughter of his uncle James, another one of Richard I's brothers. When Richard II purchased the castle and lands from his father on 1st September 1725 he was living in 'a house in Back Lane formerly called Mrs Parry's house'. Back Lane is now Belmont Road.

Richard was the deputy postmaster of Hay. He appointed John Stiffe on a salary of £25 to 'procure a man and horse to ride the stage from the Hay to the city of Hereford every Monday, Wednesday and Saturday'.[23] Perhaps understandably Richard was not universally liked. On 15 August 1734 he prosecuted Elizabeth Gwynne for causing a nuisance by 'stopping the gutter of prosecutor's mansion house'. Details unknown. The prosecution was quashed.

In 1745, like his father, he was made High Sheriff of Brecknockshire and also gave his address as Hay Castle. In 1749 Richard II was appointed Received General for the counties of Brecon, Radnor and Montgomery. This is a treasury appointment, and the person is responsible for receiving payments due to the government and making payments on its behalf.

Henry III Wellington (1719-10.9.1768).

Richard II had no children and so he was succeeded in 1760 by Henry III Wellington, the grandson of Richard I's brother Henry I.

Henry married Elizabeth on 5 January 1739, and on 28 April that year Elizabeth had a son Henry IV. He did not survive. When Henry III died, on 10 September 1768, Henry's second son Richard III inherited the castle.

Henry III and Elizabeth leased land at Llangorse to David Powell on a 999-year lease in 1743. Their son Richard III bought the lease back from David for the sum of £25 in 1781.[24]

Hay in 1741 - the castle is on the left.
Steel engraving by Henry Gastineau, 1791-1876, Public domain.
{{PD-Art|PD-old-auto-expired|deathyear=1876}}
https://archive.org/stream/walesillustrated01gast#page/n5/mode/thumb.

Richard III Wellington (1746-17.8.1808).

Richard III was a prominent citizen in the county but kept a relatively low profile. In the family tradition he was High Sheriff of Brecknockshire in 1794.[25] Richard married Penelope, (d.1.02.1792) a widow, and relict of Christopher Harris of Hayne in Devon. Her father was the Reverend Donnithorne, Cannon of Hereford.

Richard's name appeared on the list of members of the Grand Jury of 1792. This consisted of 26 prominent citizens from across Brecknockshire who sat at Brecon Assises on the six-monthly judges' rounds. In 1804 he may have still been a juror and sat at the trial of Mary Morris of Hay who was accused of infanticide for the killing of her baby daughter. This was presided over by Judge Hardinge who went to Presteigne a couple of months later and presided over the tragic case of Mary Morgan.

Both girls were found guilty of killing their newborn infants. Mary Morris of Hay was given two years in prison whereas Mary Morgan at Presteigne paid the ultimate penalty for her infanticide.[26] She was the last woman to be hanged in Radnorshire.

As a country-dwelling gentleman, with extensive land, naturally, Richard was a sporting man. During the 1790s he was issued with several Game Certificates.

Richard was one of the three executors of Whitmore Blashfield, of Hay and Cusop. Blashfield had been a tanner and owned extensive land in Kington. In January 1791 the trustees advertised asking for outstanding accounts[27] but there was a subsequent dispute with Whitmore's widow Ann. She placed an advert in 1795 stating that tithes were to be paid directly to her and threatened prosecution against anyone continuing to pay the original trustees in whom she no longer had faith.[28]

During the recent castle renovations, an interesting discovery was made in the storage area at the base of the keep. Brick wine bins had been installed here to form a wine cellar. These were always assumed to be a Victorian addition, but this has been proven to be incorrect. They were installed by the Wellingtons, probably Richard III.

When the brick vaulting was removed a void was discovered at the back of two of them. Within it were six wine bottles. Unfortunately all were empty, but they were of an early high-quality design from the time that wine was stored in reusable bottles and decanted before serving. This dates them c1760-1800, and one had the seal of Richard Wellington on it.

By the nature of where the bottles were found the supposition is that the butler would sneak down to the cellar to sample some of the contents. He would then hide the incriminating evidence by dropping the empty bottles into the void to escape detection. Fragments of several other bottles were found, all of a similar age, but not of the same 'wine cellar' quality.

A glass bottle seal of Richard Wellington found in the base of the keep from the time when it was used as a wine cellar.

Henry IV Wellington.

Henry IV was living at the castle in 1809 when he succeeded his father Richard III who followed the family tradition and died intestate. Henry was the final member of the family to live there.

The year he inherited Henry married the Honourable Charlotte Henrietta Marianna Devereux, second daughter of George Devereux 13th Viscount Hereford, sister to the 14th Viscount, Henry Devereux.[29] On 14 July 1813 Lady Wellington gave birth to a son Henry V James. Their first daughter Charlotte Marianne was born in 1816 and a second daughter Emma Julia was born on 17 January 1818 at the castle.

At this time the castle was still split into separate apartments. In 1813 a letter from Edward Jones's daughter Mary described the occupants. 'Mrs Gwyn - rather prickly. Mrs Wellington is rather plain but motherly and kind. Mr Wellington is a nice man. Lord Hereford was at the castle for two days in Easter'.[30]

Gentlemen of standing, such as Henry, were often asked to act in a responsible manner to give impartial advice or support. He was made a replacement trustee of a will in 1814 related to the sale of land at Clyro.

As a country squire he also had an active social life. He enjoyed shooting and held a Three Guinea Game-Duty Certificate in 1807 for his shooting parties. Interestingly this only covered from the first day of July to the fifth of September of the same year. The Morning Post 6 September 1810 included Mr Wellington in its list of 'Fashionable Departures' from London for Hereford, and Hay Castle.

In 1805 he placed an advertisement for his horse, 'Pretender' to cover the 1806 season, described as:

'a bright bay horse only four years old fifteen hands and one inch high.
Pretender was got by Old Pretender, well known in Herefordshire, and his dam
Old Bridgenorth Snap'.
Available at Hay Castle Breconshire. Mares at two guineas and half a crown the groom.[31]

For at least 200 years a secure cellar at the castle had been used as a 'lock-up' by the local bailiffs and police force. Conscious of how unsatisfactory this was, in 1810 Henry obtained possession of the derelict St John's Chantry Chapel in the centre of Hay. He instructed John Milward to convert it into a new lock-up with two cells, for no more than £151. This then provided the town's custodial provision until a new police station was built in 1875. Subsequently the old lock-up had a variety of different uses such as butchers, hairdressers, and a school.

In 1930 part of this building was converted back into a new St John's Chapel at the instigation of Mary Louise Dawson, eldest daughter of Rev. William Latham Bevan, a later tenant of Hay Castle.

For some reason, in 1821, Henry IV and Charlotte decided to move from Hay. Henry advertised 'all that commodious and desirable mansion, called Hay Castle' as available to let on a term of seven years. The accommodation was described as:

> *'consisting of an entrance hall, a dining room, drawing room, gentleman's morning room with dressing-room attached, five excellent bed chambers, two dressing rooms, nursery and large airy attics for servants; kitchen, butlers-pantry, larder, servants-hall, dairy, cellars, and all.*
> *Inferior and necessary offices, double coach house and good stabling'.*[32]

There were also two acres of garden, a fine salmon run within a few hundred yards of the house, and 18 acres of meadow land on offer.[33]

Henry let his part of the castle to Joseph Bailey almost immediately. While the accommodation appears to have been substantial it can only have been part of it as reputedly Joseph Bailey had already leased some of it in 1809.

Henry put his furniture up for auction on 1 November 1821. A few years later there was another auction, this time at the Swan Hotel. This may have been residual items not sold in 1821 or from another of the units at the castle which had become vacant.

The second auction description stated that it consisted of furniture from 'the Mansion House, Hay Castle, late of Henry Wellington'.[34] This wording usually suggests someone has died but Henry Wellington 'of Hay Castle' subsequently travelled extensively. He was at Honfleur in France in 1844, and with Charlotte in Exmouth when she predeceased him on 27 May 1861 aged 86 years.

Henry himself died on 20 September 1868 aged 89 years. He was at St Bernard's, Southsea, in the home of his daughter Emma and son-in-law the Rev. L.H. St George, chaplain to H.M. forces. Henry and Charlotte now lie together in Glasbury churchyard.

Their eldest daughter Charlotte Marianne Wellington did not marry. It is assumed but not known if she travelled with her parents. She died on 25 June 1898 at Kensington Palace Mansions aged 82 years.

Henry V James Wellington.

Henry V only lived at the castle as a child. In 1825 shortly after the family left Hay 12-year-old Henry V joined the Navy. By 1831 he was a midshipman on HMS Rainbow in Malta and was promoted to commander on 12 Aug 1834. When Richard married Emma Jane Ireland on 10 October 1843 he was registered on HMS Queen at Portsmouth.

Although still a commander in October 1867 when he retired, he was promoted on leaving the service to the rank of retired captain. Henry V was the Henry Wellington of Hay described as owning 21 acres, worth a rental income of £122 p.a., in the Breconshire 'Doomsday Book' of 1876.[35]

In 1846 his youngest daughter Emma Julia, aged 28 years, married Leonard Henry St. George son of Lieut. Col. George Durant of Tong Castle at Poole in Dorset.

Legal Case.

A high-profile legal case in Hereford had a peripheral connection to the castle but confirms that the Gwynne family retained a connection during the time of the Wellington occupation.

In 1819 Thynne Howell Gwynne of Buckland Hall, Brecon brought an action for damages against his cousin Colonel Sackville Frederick Gwynne of Glanbran, Carmarthenshire. Thynne accused Sackville of 'improper correspondence' with his wife Georgina, a sister of Lord Hereford. He even proposed a duel over the issue but this was declined by Sackville.

At one stage in the relationship, there was a meeting to investigate the circumstances related to an anonymous letter believed to have been written by Sackville to Georgina. This was convened at Thynne's suggestion by Lord Hereford at Hay Castle, the home of his other sister Charlotte.

Following the meeting, a letter signed by Colonel Charles Cornwall, Jnr. of Moccas Court, J.B. Cheston, Georgina's brother-in-law, and W. Watkins, possibly the Parliamentary officer William Watkins of Penyrwrlodd, Llanigon, concluded Georgina was guilty of 'great indiscretion' but 'does not prove to our minds that any criminality has taken part between the parties'.

They suggested if Thynne is satisfied with her 'professions of sincere penitence' he should take his wife back. This was accompanied by a letter from Georgina professing such penitence and promising never to contact Sackville again. Both letters are dated Hay Castle, Nov 17, 1817.

Subsequently, Georgina broke her promise and so the case came to court where Thynne sought £20,000 in damages from Sackville. The jury found for Thynne but only awarded him £1,000.[36]

Chapter 3 - Hay Vicarage.

Castle occupancy following Henry IV Wellington's departure is confusing, compounded by the splitting of the lordship of the manor of Hay from the ownership of the castle.

Henry seems to have been a part owner, together with members of the Gwynn family – Walter and William, and the Hon. Roach Gwynn. Roach married the Hon. Rev. John Harley who owned the lordship. They moved into the castle in 1771 but by 1791 John was dean of Windsor so how long they resided there is unknown.

For the next 130 years the castle then had multiple ecclesiastical occupants.

- The **Rev. Williams Allen** had been appointed as vicar of Hay in 1786 but was only active in his ecclesiastical duties in the town from 1824-27. On 2 November 1826 'Catherine, 4th daughter of Rev. W. Allen of Hay Castle' died after a short illness.[1] She was buried at Glasbury, aged 23 years.

    On that basis the Rev. Williams might only have moved into the castle shortly before his daughter's death. That was about the same time that it was reported 'Last week some persons entered the Castle, at the Hay, and stole two beds, with the bedclothes and hangings'.[2]

- In 1827, following Rev. Williams Allen, **Rev. Walter Wilkins**, (1782-1851), was appointed to St Mary's, Hay. He married Anna Maria Jacoba, (1783-1837) daughter of Lorenzo Chiappini and sister of Lady Newborough, on 5 September 1809 in Italy. They took up residence as tenants of the castle on 16 April 1828.[3]

    Their first three children Walter (1812-53) Frances (1813-57) and Thomas (1814-1902) were born in Cusop, their middle child Charles (b1819) in Florence, and the last three, Catherine (1821-1916), Henry (1823-95) and John (1827-34) in Hay, while their father was still vicar of Boughrood.

- o Thomas joined the Royal Horse Artillery and served in Canada. On the death of his father in 1851 he moved back and settled in Gloucestershire. Later he was a magistrate in Breconshire and Gloucester.[4]
- o Charles son, also called Charles, joined the Hampshire Regiment and was wounded at Gallipoli.[5]
- o Henry became the vicar of Boughrood.

- In 1836 Rev. Wilkins took out a lease of the castle for another year. The extensive Wilkins family changed their name to de Winton in 1839 and the Rev. de Winton was living in Clyro in 1841. He was the vicar of Llanigon and Bronllys and living at Llanstephan House in 1851 at the time of his death.[6]

- From the mid-1830s the **Rev. Richard Allen,** closely followed by the **Rev. Richard Venables**, were appointed as Hay Union Workhouse Guardians. They did not stop long, and there is no record that they resided at the castle.

- In 1831 the **Rev. Humphrey Allen**, aged 40, became the first stipendiary (paid, and licenced by the bishop) curate of Hay. Eight years later he was appointed a surrogate for marriage licences by the bishop of St David's.

Rev. Allen was the son of barrister Sir Henry Allen of Glasbury, and his son had considerable private means, including a field at Westbrook. He moved into the castle, at a rent of £50pa., with his wife the Hon. Ann Caroline Allen (nee Fitzroy), 35 years. She was the sister-in-law of the third Baron Southampton. In 1841 the Allens employed five servants: Mary Jane Broad, 30, Susan Powell, 25, Mary Ann Challenger, 20, George Gough, 36 and James Griffiths, 20.

They were a very popular couple and strong supporters of any attempts to improve the town. When it was proposed that gas lighting be installed in Hay Rev. Allen donated a piece of land off Newport Road for the gasworks. He then became the principal shareholder in the new company. When the National School in Brecon Road was built it had a deficiency of £500. The benevolent curate contributed approximately a third of this to help clear the debt.

In 1839 he 'kindly permitted himself to be referred to' about the new school being set up by the Misses Dyke in a 'large and commodious house in the pleasant and healthy Town of Hay'. Each pupil was required to bring a 'silver dessert and teaspoon'.[7]

Humphrey was a strong supporter of the Church Missionary Society and frequently attended their meetings at the Shire Hall, Presteigne, a journey of 20 miles from Hay, by horse-drawn carriage or on horseback. In support of the society, he preached in Crickhowell, Abergavenny and Swansea.

What precipitated the vicar's thoughts of leaving his parish is unknown, but it became a matter of concern to his parishioners. A memorial published in July 1843 beseeched him to stay 'after nineteen years it has pleased God so prominently to bless your exertions'. The memorial contained over 500 signatures 'affixed in the short space of two days'.[8]

Notorious Hay solicitor James Spencer published a letter a week later pointing out that four of the signatories were deceased, many were parishioners from outside Hay i.e. Cusop and Clyro, and a number were under the age of 18 years, 12 years, or inmates of the Union Workhouse. He further accused the Reverend of not wanting to leave and instigating the memorial himself. What the full story was behind this we do not know.[9]

A follow-up letter by John Williams of the Thatched Tavern in Hay appeared a week later. He claimed his name and that of his children were on the memorial despite his refusing to sign it. He suggested the Rev. gentleman should ignore the list, consisting mostly of women and children. Instead, he should take notice of the ratepayers in the town, of whom 'the greater part would be for your going'.[10] Local politics!

Rev. Allen agreed to reconsider his decision, but three years later on 22 January 1844, he sold his furniture from the castle. He left at the end of February possibly because he felt obliged to move following criticism of him in providing a character reference and support to Hay Police Supt. William McMahon.

In a sensational complicated case, McMahon was found guilty on a charge of assault. For this, he received one month's custody at Brecon and a £5 fine. After the month was over he returned to Hay, but a mob attacked the postmaster's house he was staying in.

The house was on the corner of Oxford Road and Castle/Church Street only a short distance from the castle. The Rev. Allen hurried down and attempted to defend McMahon. For his trouble he was on the receiving end of a bombardment of stones. At a subsequent trial related to perjury during the assault case, McMahon was sentenced to seven years transportation, although he was subsequently pardoned.[11]

Rev. Allen left Hay in 1844 but he still described himself as 'of the Hay' in an action brought by him and Charles Williams Allen of the Moor, Cusop, as well as three others, in London. This was an application to the Privy Council for an extension to a patent for 'certain improvements in the manufacture of woollen and other fabrics' and the associated machinery to achieve this. Possibly he had not thought to update his previous prestigious address.

Rev. Allen as curate may have aspired to be the vicar of Hay in succession to the absentee vicar William Bowen, but he did not get the opportunity. When William Bowen died in 1845 and the living became vacant it was offered elsewhere. Possibly the McMahon incident made the curate persona non grata in the town. More likely it was due to Joseph Bailey's nepotism.

Joseph Bailey.

Joseph Bailey was the successful ironmaster at the Nant-y-glo Works, a business he purchased in 1817. Joseph and his brother Crawshaw increased production to five blast furnaces in 1823 and later increased this to seven.

The Nant y glo ironworks, Monmouthshire. Public domain.
Steel engravings from works by Gastineau, Henry, 1791-1876.
{{PD-Art|PD-old-auto-expired|deathyear=1876}}
https://archive.org/stream/walesillustrated01gast#page/n5/mode/thumb.

When he retired in 1830, having made his fortune, he and Crawshaw jointly bought a number of estates throughout Brecknock, Radnorshire, Monmouthshire and Glamorganshire. Hay was not one of those.

Meanwhile, an auction held at the Hotel Hereford on the 14 October 1826 was for 'The extensive and valuable Freehold Manor of English Hay, with tolls, rents etc. + land and properties on 720 acres'.[12] It seems that this sale of the manor (it did not include the castle) was not very popular, or perhaps not viewed to be of sufficient value, as the auction was unsuccessful.

On 9 June 1827 the 'Freehold Manor of Hay' was put up for auction again, with the same description, this time at the Swan Inn, Hay.[13] The auction was repeated with the same advert on 28 June 1828, and again at the Swan Inn.[14]

The following year on 11 June the advertisement was shorter. 'The Manor or Lordship of English Hay with tolls, rents etc', also at the Swan Inn. It is not clear what was included in the annual value given as £77.00.[15]

On 6 May 1833, Joseph Bailey purchased the Lordship of the Manor from the Right Hon. Edward Harley Earl of Oxford and Earl Mortimer. The first year Joseph held court as the Lord of the Manor was in 1833. He was knighted in 1852.[16]

Separately, in 1844 at the time the Rev. Allen left Hay, the castle was put up for sale.

SALES BY AUCTION.

Breconshire and Herefordshire.—By Messrs. FAREBROTHER and Co., at the Swan Hotel, in the Town of Hay, on Friday, Oct. 7, at Three in the Afternoon, in Thirteen Lots,

VERY VALUABLE FREEHOLD ESTATES,

adjoining the town of Hay, in Breconshire; consisting of the distinguished residence, known as

HAY CASTLE,

with offices, coach-house and stabling, beautiful lawn, garden, and pleasure-grounds and shrubbery; the whole about 2a 1r 17p, seated upon a fine eminence, commanding extensive highly-picturesque scenery; let to the Rev. H. Allen until February next. An

EXTENSIVE AND WELL-PLANTED GARDEN,

and four pieces of rich meadow land, called Cae Mawr, Upper and Lower Cae Bach, and Cae Mawr Plock; let to Messrs. Hope, Biddle, Vincent, and others. A cottage and garden, and four pieces of excellent meadow land, called Cardigan Hall and Green Pit Lands; let to William Jones and Samuel Evans. A cottage and garden, and piece of meadow land; let to William Price. And a plot of building ground adjoining the turnpike road to Hereford, and several gardens adjoining.

The original advertisement appeared on 29 December 1843. In addition to extensive grounds and various pieces of meadowland, a detailed description of the accommodation was given.

- Upper floor.
    - 6 bedrooms.

- First floor.
    - capital bedroom   20 ft sq.
    - another bedroom 20ft x 10ft.
    - another bedroom 23ft sq. and dressing room.
    - another bedroom.

- Elizabethan staircase leading to the fine old tower (now known as the keep).

- Ground floor.
    - Porch entrance.
    - Spacious hall paved floor 30ft x 20ft, library, gentleman's dressing room and china closet.
    - Inner hall, light oak staircase, and water closet.

- A cheerful drawing room about 22ft sq. elegantly papered and fitted with a marble chimneypiece.

- A capital dining room 22ft x 16 ft with recess for a sideboard, neatly papered and fitted with marble chimneypiece.

- Back staircase.

- Offices: housekeeper's room, butler's pantry, kitchen, back kitchen, servant's hall, laundry, and excellent cellarage.

- Back yard: bake and brew houses, dairy, larder, and other buildings.

- Paved carriage yard with four stalled stable and loft over, coach house for four carriages, loose box with loft over.

Coach house and stables at Hay Castle built by Joseph Bailey.
Photograph by the author.

In October 1844 the castle owners, Thynne Howell Gwynne and Henry IV Wellington, sold it to ironmaster Joseph Bailey of Glanusk Park, M.P. for Worcester from 1835 and then Brecknock from 1847.

Joseph had rented part of the castle, possibly from 1806, certainly from 1833, and in 1844 he paid £826 to buy the whole site. Under him, the lordship and castle ownership were united once more.

At this time the castle was in a neglected and dilapidated state. Joseph proceeded to spend a considerable sum of money to ensure that it was 'put into complete repair'.[17] His work included amalgamating all the separate (Wellington) 'apartments' into one unified unit of accommodation.

Outside he was also responsible for building the stables and coach house and coupled with this he is believed to have created the circular carriage drive. It is also possible that he built the wall edging the bottom lawn behind the Honesty Bookshop shelves fronting Castle Street.[18]

Although Joseph spent a great deal of money to put the site in a good state of repair, he did not need the castle as a home. His main residence was on the estate he bought at Crickhowell in 1826. There he had the prestigious property Glanusk Park built, designed by Robert Lugar and garden designer Arthur Markham Nesfield.

An image of the keep by John George Wood 1816.
Public Domain. National Library of Wales.[19]

The missing corner of the keep tower of Hay Castle has intrigued visitors for years. How did it get like that? The Wood engraving of 1816 shows the tower was crumbling from neglect but essentially intact. On that basis, it could not have been damaged in any of the Anglo-Welsh skirmishes in the 12th, 13th or 14th centuries. The conjecture is that Joseph demolished the corner to 'beautify' it and make it look like a picturesque ruin in the Victorian fashion.

The Bailey family then continued to own Hay Castle for 90 years during which time it passed from Joseph to his successors. They also did not live in it. First, his grandson Sir Joseph Russell Bailey, who later became 1st Baron Glanusk, inherited in 1858. In 1906 he was succeeded by the 2nd Baron Joseph Henry Russell Bailey. Finally, Wilfred Russell Bailey inherited it in 1928 and sold it eight years later. During all this time it went through a relatively stable period of occupation, with only three tenants from 1845 to 1935.

Rev. William Latham Bevan.

Rev. William Latham Bevan. Available under
https://en.wikipedia.org/wiki/en:Creative_Commons.

As Lord of the Manor Joseph Bailey held the patronage of the living at St Mary's Church. This was one of five eventually held by 1st Lord Glanusk, the descendant of Joseph Bailey.[20] Joseph decided to offer it to his nephew Rev. William Latham Bevan who had recently been ordained and was at that time a curate in London. Financially this was not a sound appointment. Hay parish had little income and there was no vicarage. However, in offering the living, Joseph was prepared to allow the use of the mansion at Hay Castle as the rectory for the nominal rent of £20 a year.

William was the son of the sister of Joseph's first wife Maria. William's father William Hibbs Bevan was half of Kendal and Bevan who operated the Beaufort Iron Works, and High Sheriff of Brecknock in 1841. He had three sons William Latham, Henry Bailey and George Phillips, and one daughter Margaret Ann Ellen.

William Latham Bevan was born on 1 May 1821 at Beaufort, Llangattock. Like his brothers, he went to Rugby School, William under the famous Dr Thomas Arnold whose son Matthew was a contemporary. William matriculated at Balliol College in 1838, Magdalene (now Hertford) College, Oxford, for his Batchelor's in 1842 and then Master of Arts degree in 1845. At Magdalene he was awarded the Lusby open scholarship in classics.

His brother Henry Bailey Bevan J.P. went to Merton College Oxford before being ordained in 1851 at St David's Cathedral. He held assistant curacies at Brecon, then in Hay with his brother William in 1851, and later at Tretower near Crickhowell. He retired early due to ill health. In the 1881 census, ten years before his death, he was described as a 'clergyman without cure of souls'.

William's youngest brother George Phillips Bevan obtained the Diploma of the Royal College of Surgeons in 1850 and for a time was the doctor at his father's ironworks at Beaufort before abandoning medicine for a literary career.

A Fellow of the Royal Statistical Society and the Geological Society of London he was a multi-talented statistician, geographer, and editor. His popular tourist guides covered Hampshire, Surrey, Kent, Ridings of Yorkshire, Warwickshire, the Wye Valley and the Channel Islands. A Handbook to St Pauls Cathedral and a series on "British Manufacturing Industries' were also his.

William Bevan the Churchman.[21]

On 2 June 1844, the Rev. W.L. Bevan was licensed a deacon by the Lord Bishop of London and admitted into holy orders. After a curacy at St Philips Stepney for a few months in 1845, he moved to Hay, serving the parish, and living in the castle, for the next 56 years.

Rev. Bevan followed the Anglican High Church tradition and was strongly anti-Catholic. A highly respected churchman in Wales, he was cool, critical, and dispassionate, very un-Welsh.

During his long career he was given several additional appointments. These include becoming Rural Dean, prebendary of Llandewi (1876-79) and canon prebendary of St David's cathedral (1879-93). He was offered at least four Welsh Deaneries but turned them down so that he could continue to live in Hay. He was chaplain to the Hay Union Workhouse 1850-95.

Appointed archdeacon of Brecon in 1895 he retired to Ely Tower at Brecon Cathedral in November 1901. Rev. Bevan remained archdeacon until 1907, shortly before he died when his son Rev. Edward Latham Bevan succeeded him to the post.

Although born in Wales the archdeacon was not a fiery Welshman. A dogged fighter for the established church in Wales, he was a hard-headed Victorian. Unemotional and dispassionate, with a remote demeanour but widely respected and loved by his parishioners. Little is known about his early years in Hay, but from the start his private income meant the castle could become his home.

With such a large house he must have required a number of servants. We do not have any details of these in the early years, except that on 13 February 1849 the Hereford Journal published a notice of the death at Hay Castle of Mrs Charlotte Haydon, aged 55 years, faithful servant and housekeeper to Rev. W.L. Bevan.

The Bevan Family at Hay Castle.

On 19 July 1849 William married Louisa, the third daughter of Tomkyns Dew of Whitney Court, where she was born in 1821.

> *'Seventeen handsome equipages conveyed the wedding party to the church and there were ten bridesmaids … in the small, retired village of Whitney there is scarcely an inhabitant who will not in their future years, recall the impressive spectacle.*[22]

The newly married couple settled at the castle, which was given the address Horse Fair, Hay, in the 1851 census. Horse Fair was the road outside the castle gates going down to the Castle Street junction, and where the annual horse fair was held.

The castle provided an ideal home for William and Louisa to raise their large family, and a centre for the archdeacon to conduct his parish affairs.

Rev. W.L. Bevan with his family in 1895.
Photograph courtesy Hay Castle Trust.

Louisa Bevan (1821-18.09.1908).

Details of Bevan family life are sparse, but it appears to have been a very happy active household, albeit typically Victorian in its attitude towards bringing up children. Examples include half an egg being quite sufficient for a child's breakfast, and never allowing butter and jam to be eaten together. Regardless all the family appear to have been happy and supportive of one another.

Charity played a key role at the vicarage, and Louisa, as the vicar's wife, was involved in multiple charitable works. When the church was reopened in 1867 after the new chancel was built, paid for by her husband, Louisa made and decorated the cushions in front of the altar rail.

Unfortunately, the extent of her charity work was limited by her health. Despite, or because of, having seven children she was something of an invalid. In his diaries the Rev. Francis Kilvert often alluded to her indisposition when he visited.

It seems Louisa was popular, just unable to participate in pastoral life as much as she might like. Her daughter Mary fulfilled much of this role until she left for Yorkshire when in her early 40s.

Following the marriage of their second daughter Alice, 'Mrs Bevan of Hay Castle', provided a recommendation for the Belle Vue Restaurant Co. Her letter published in the Weston Super Mare Gazette said that she and Canon Bevan would recommend 'Mr George to any friends' to provide 'hall suppers or wedding breakfasts'. 'She was very pleased with the efficiency and excellent conduct of the men who came with the breakfast'.[23] Naturally the wedding was in St Mary's Church Hay with the breakfast at the castle.

- **Mary Louisa (1.12.1850-21.10.1932).**

Mary was born at Crickhowell. As she grew up Francis Kilvert described her as 'radiant with her beautiful eyes and brow'. On another occasion, he said, 'she looked very pretty in her white-feathered hat and red and black check cloak'. Amongst her good works was being a Sunday school teacher, and supporting the Girls Friendly Society.

No recluse, Mary had an active social life in Herefordshire, and she liked to flirt in the company of military officers when the family were staying at Weymouth.

For her time Mary was extremely well educated and she was 'thoroughly Welsh by nature, passionately devoted to the Welsh country and country people and the Welsh traditions'.[24] She was also an expert on Welsh saints. Always dressed all in black she had the reputation as a witch.[25]

As well as translating Celtic poetry Mary was something of a poet. In the winter of 1879, the family stayed at San Remo where they met Edward Lear the noted author. Mary and Edward wrote a poem together starting 'How pleasant to know Mr Lear', and Mary was sent a copy complete with a drawing by Edward.

In 1883 she married Lt Col Henry Phillip Dawson R.A., and to mark the occasion the town raised the money to present her with a silver salver. The couple lived at the castle for a further six years, where their daughter and son were born. Henry continued in the army but on being drafted to Singapore in 1896 he decided to retire. They went to live at Harlington Hall in the Craven part of the Yorkshire Dales, a Dawson ancestral property for over 200 years.

Their second child Henry Christopher Dawson was born on 12 October 1889 and became a famous Catholic philosopher and a leading Catholic historian. He took up teaching posts at Exeter, Liverpool, Edinburgh and Harvard Universities. The first six years of his life were spent at the castle, an upbringing which imbued him with a strong sense of history, and timelessness as his mother had been raised there as well. After moving to Yorkshire Christopher always felt that his mother 'missed Wales and the closely integrated family life of Hay and the Welsh border'.[26]

Mary had a strong religious streak and developed an interest in St John's Guild Chapel in Hay. Originally this was the medieval Guild Chapel Iron or Evan (Welsh for John) for the town tradesmen and was founded in 1254. The chapel was later used by the occupants of the castle mansion. It fell into disrepair before becoming the town lock-up.

After the opening of the new police station in 1875 it had a variety of uses including a fire station, hairdressers, and butchers. Late in life, Mary wrote the history of the chapel before acquiring the building in 1929. She then had it rebuilt into a new small chapel and several meeting rooms before presenting it to the parish. The bell-cote contains a bell inscribed Edward Wellington CW 1718.

The chapel was consecrated by her brother Edward, Lord Bishop of the new Diocese of Swansea and Brecon, on Friday 10 October 1930. By now Mary was 80 years old and too ill to attend in person so she was represented by her daughter Gwendoline.[27]

- **Alice Catherine (1853-17.2.1925).**

Alice was born in Hay and married Captain Thomas Llewellyn Morgan (d.17.1.1921), a captain in the Royal Horse Artillery, on 14 August 1883. The ceremony was in Hay. Thomas was from the family on the St Helens Estate, Swansea. They lived for a short time at Buckingham House, Brecon, before moving to Oakfield House, Hay.

In 1916 they moved to the Poole area of Hereford, and on her husband's death in 1921, Alice moved to 'Greenhill', Weymouth. Alice and Thomas had one son Jeffrey and a daughter Sibell.

Alice was one of those who supported the restoration of the Courvoisier's Chapel in Brecon Cathedral, for women's services and in memory of her sister Ellen. She donated the organ.

- Frances Emily Lewis (28.9.1853-23.1.1945).

Frances was born in Hay and married the Rev. David Lewis Davies, Rector of Vaynor, Merthyr Tydfil in June 1897. She was very popular, and three hundred Hay residents signed a testimonial to her. They presented 'a massive silver inkstand and blotter, envelope case, a case of dessert knives and forks, and a case of fish knives and forks.

Independent of this over one hundred guests presented a vast quantity and variety of gifts including numerous silver cutlery items, including multiple fish knives and forks, silver dishes, crockery, lamps, furniture, clocks, linen and lace ware. Her sister Ellen gave her a sapphire and diamond ring.

The members of the Girls Friendly Society sent 'a massive gold curb bracelet with a gold padlock bearing the bride's monogram…'.

- (William) Armine (1855-1938).

Armine was born in Hay and married Amy Henriette Wayet on 22 August 1885 at Clifton in Bristol. Her dress was of rich ivory white satin, with a long train, and an embroidered pearl front.

> *'She wore a wreath of orange blossom in her hair*
> *and a tulle veil held back with pearl pins*
> *and she carried a bouquet of stephanotis eucharis lilies*
> *and white blossoms given by the bridegroom.'*[28]

Armine was a businessman with varied interests, including trading with South Africa at one time. He was director of the National Agricultural Hall Company Limited Kensington (Olympia) in 1886 when it offered 10,000 shares at £10 a share. The Hippodrome of Paris was to be their opening show from which they expected large profits.[29] Armine was also the president of Newcastle Breweries in the 1890s when the company underwent a massive, profitable, expansion.

His will, made on 15 February 1932, included the exhortation 'to prepare for a war which I believe to be inevitable within fifteen years unless a proper navy and an adequate army is maintained'. It was widely quoted in the press.

In later life he was a keen supporter of the arts and many artists, singers and actors benefitted from his will.

- Frederick (19-20.06.1859).

Their second son Frederick was born on 19 June 1859 but unfortunately only lived for one day.

- Ellen (1858-15.04.1921).

Ellen was born in Hay. She never married and her life appears to have consisted to a large extent of participation in the charity events that defined her family. Ellen was a regular flower lady at the church and frequently won first prize in the cut flower section of the Hay Flower Show.

A typical event was in 1896 when Ellen sang in a musical show given to a Mothers Meeting, the mothers of the Sunday and day school children, after a celebration tea. For many years she acted as secretary to the Hay branch of the Church of England Temperance Society, founded by her brother Edward in 1881. She cut the cake on its 25th anniversary. Ellen also donated an enamelled silver badge, for good conduct and regular attendance, to the St Mary's Band of Hope.

After moving to Brecon with her parents when her father retired Ellen went with her mother to Melcombe Regis in 1901.

On her death, Ellen was buried in St Keynes Chapel, formerly Courvoisier's Chapel St John's Priory Church Brecon, after it was redesigned by W.D. Caroe the famous ecclesiastical architect. The chapel was dedicated to the Mothers Union, Girls Friendly Society and women's work in the arch deanery in Ellen's memory.

- Edward Latham (27.10.1861-2.02.1934).

Teddy was the Bevan's second living son. He was born and eventually died in Melcombe Regis Weymouth. After studying at his father's old college at Oxford and attending Wells Theological College he was appointed curate at Holy Trinity, Weymouth, from 1886 to 91.

For a time he worked abroad, electing to go to Khartoum. On his return, he founded a Gordon Boys School in Weymouth. This organisation had been set up to commemorate General Gordon of Khartoum. The school taught boys from poor backgrounds useful skills such as carpentry, blacksmithing, tailoring and engineering. From 1891 to 1897 he was chaplain to the school.

The Rev. Edward Latham Bevan was appointed vicar of Brecon in 1897 and a member of the Brecon Board of Guardians for the workhouse. Other appointments included rural dean and archdeacon in 1907 on the retirement of his father, and he became the last Bishop Suffragan of Swansea in 1915. In 1921 he was appointed the first bishop of the newly formed diocese of Swansea and Brecon.

As the Brecknock Battalion South Wales Borderers chaplain from 1902, he accompanied them on numerous annual camps with his refreshment, reading and writing tent. In 1915 he went with them to Aden, and the following year returned to accompany them for a time at Mhow in India.

Like his father, Edward had a strong interest in education and was a member of the Breconshire Education Committee from 1908. He never married.

As bishop he received a great deal of correspondence. His sense of humour was always tickled when he received letters to 'Bishop of Swansea, Esq', or 'Messrs Swansea and Brecon'. A portrait of him hangs in the National Portrait Gallery London.

Weymouth.

The Bevan's had strong connections with Melcombe Regis and Weymouth. In 1871 they were at 6 Pulteney Buildings, part of the elegant Georgian facade on the esplanade at Melbourne Regis, a part of Weymouth. In 1844 this had been a boarding house, but its later status is unknown.

The family were connected with the area for many years. In 1901 Louisa was at 5 Victoria Terrace, Melcombe with her daughter Ellen. As previously described Edward was born, worked as a curate, founded and was chaplain to the Gordon School, and eventually died in Weymouth. After Alice was widowed in 1921, she retired to Weymouth.

Servants.

A large Victorian vicarage with a big family required servants. Four live-in servants were normally employed. Over the years there were a continuous variety of lady's maids, parlour maids and kitchen maids, always a cook, and when the children were young a nurse. During the 1870s the nursing role was replaced by a lady's maid.

The only male servant known was 16-year-old William Coxall, employed in 1851. His role is unknown. There would have been additional servants who lived out, such as a gardener, groom and later a driver.

The family was resident at Pulteney Melcombe Regis during the census of 1871, when they had two servants who accompanied the family down from Hay. Rosetta Selig aged 26 years was a governess, born in Gloucester, and Sarah (Jane) Crump aged 41 years was a nurse, born in Bodenham, Herefordshire. Sarah died in 1900 aged 76 years after 43 years of service.

In 1901 there was additional help, perhaps understandable as Louisa would have been 80 years old by now. Her nurse/lady's maid was in addition to a parlourmaid, housemaid, kitchen maid and cook.

That year Louisa went to Melcombe with Ellen, and nurse Eliza Williams as support.

Reverend Francis Kilvert.

The diaries of Francis Kilvert the famous Clyro curate give some idea of life in the Victorian vicarage of an influential churchman who had a large family. Kilvert was a frequent visitor and describes a stream of occasions when he was specifically invited, but also many when he just seems to have called in, been given lunch and then gone on his way.[30]

The way he describes his visits shows he was always made welcome and that there were frequently other visitors present. Primarily they were local inhabitants although there were sometimes visiting clergy staying.

The four Bevan sisters Mary, Alice, Frances, and Ellen, appear to have been an attraction for his visits. A typical occasion was the 3 July 1870 when they all gathered around the Bevington organ in the small hall and sang 'Pilgrims of the Night'. This hall with the organ overlooked the town and sometimes the family would leave the door open to allow the music to drift out.

The archdeacon's son Edward donated this hand-pumped organ to Brecon Cathedral where he became bishop. In 1971 it was restored, converted to electricity, and returned to the cathedral on a wheeled base but retaining many of its quirkier characteristics. It is still present there today.

On the 4 September 1871 Kilvert was invited to a croquet party. While he had a 'slow game of croquet' the main object of his interest, Daisy Thomas, went with Fanny Bevan to play archery in the field beyond the orchard (now the main Hay car park). Kilvert had approached Daisy's father expressing an interest in his daughter but had been told in no uncertain terms to forget her. She was not destined to marry an impoverished curate.

On 29 June the following year, archery was again the activity when Kilvert went with 'four pretty girl archers' onto the field to pick up their arrows. Ellen was an enthusiastic toxophilite and a member of Wye-Side Bowmen. She won 'Best Gold' in their meeting of July 1886.

Two months later on 28 August he was invited for dinner and received presents of a 'splendid photographic album' and a painting of heart ease.

Visits were occasions for gossip. On 4 July 1870, he found a Mrs and Miss Allen in attendance, and Mrs Bevan lying ill on a sofa. He then recounted a visit the previous week when a Mr Lyne made a spectacle of himself with his actions.

As a curate, it would be natural for him to refer to such an eminent churchman as Archdeacon Bevan, although he does not mention this specifically. Some visits coincided with the arrival of other clergy, such as Bishop McDougall back from Labuan (Malaysia). He was invited to stay overnight on many occasions despite living less than a mile away. The invitations continued after he had been appointed the vicar, and moved, to St Harmans, Bredwardine.

The Archdeacon at his jubilee celebration on the front drive of Hay Castle in 1895. Photograph courtesy of Hay Castle Trust.

Later years.

In 1895 to celebrate the Archdeacon's golden jubilee of his time in the town Louisa held a large garden party on the lawns of the castle. Almost everyone from the town attended, such was their esteem for their beloved vicar. Photographs taken at the time are an invaluable record of how the castle looked before the restyling of the property 15 years later by Dowager Lady Glanusk.

Like many Victorian country vicars, as he grew older Rev. Bevan became more autocratic. Only certain families were permitted to use the front door of the castle, and boys were expected to raise their cap or girls to curtsey when passing him in the street.

Despite this, and his strong evangelical views, he seems to have maintained good relations with his flock and the non-conformist clergy with whom he was happy to work on joint ventures.

After 56 active years, in November 1901 Archdeacon Bevan retired and moved to Brecon. The living in Hay was always poorly remunerated, and things had not improved. On his retirement, it was pointed out that after paying his curate the parish income barely amounted to £30 a year.

Fortunately he had private means and even after raising a large family, and his philanthropy in the town, he still left £100,000 in his will. He died on 21 August 1908 and is buried with his wife Louisa, who died on 23 October the following year, in Hay cemetery. In 1910 his family dedicated oak choir stalls and a marble pavement in St Mary's Church in his memory.

Philanthropic Work.

The reputation of the castle meant it was held in high esteem far and wide. In 1863 the Cambrian Archaeological Association held a four-day conference in Kington. Each day they toured part of the neighbouring area. On their final day, they made an excursion along the Wye passing through Almeley, Winforton and Clifford to Hay Castle where Rev. Bevan gave them a guided tour.

During his time in the town, Rev. Bevan was noted for his zeal in supporting the community.

- Managing the Hay branch of the Brecon Savings Bank. This opened on Thursdays from 1-2 pm in Broad Street. The Rev. Francis Kilvert covered business for him on 7 April 1870.
- Financing and building the parish rooms in Lion Street.
- Financing and building the new extended chancel of St Mary's Church in 1867.
- Member of the Workhouse Board of Guardians and Local Board.
- A stalwart of the Temperance Society.
- He was called upon to chair numerous committees and charitable institutions, as well as becoming president of numerous organisations or events such as the Hay Flower Show.

It may have been the influence of the famous Dr Arnold of Rugby but Rev. Bevan's two abiding interests were religion and education.

Religion.

A noted expert on religion in Wales he proposed the splitting of the St David's Diocese into three. After his death it was split in two and his son Teddy became the first bishop of the new Swansea and Brecon Diocese.

His publications on Welsh religious history included:

- Our Parish Church and its Endowments: St. Peters. Carmarthen. A Kessinger reprint (1884).
- A reply to H. Richard's letter to the Daily News on the Church in Wales. Kessinger Legacy (1885).
- Diocesan History St David's, Society for Promoting Christian Knowledge, London (1888).
- Various pamphlets and papers on the Welsh Church including The Church Defence Handy Volume (1892) and Notes on the Church in Wales (1905). There are translations and notes in his handwriting in Brecon Museum related to St John's Chapel Hay.
- Smith's Dictionary of the Bible.

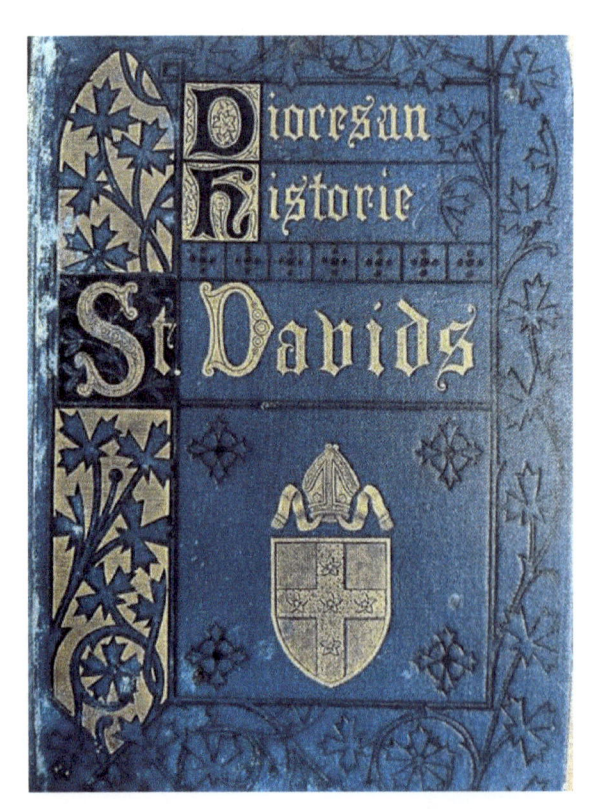

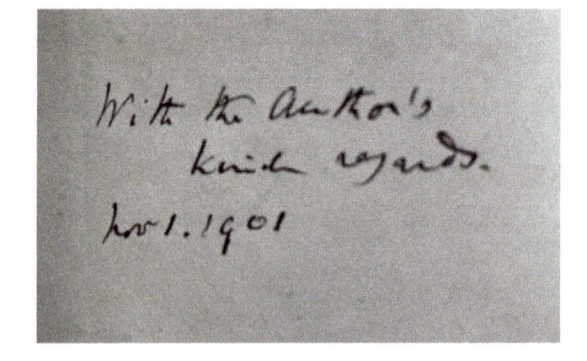

Bevan and Education.

Rev. Bevan had an academic mind and was fluent in Latin and Greek from his school days, but also in French, German, Dutch, and Norwegian. He had a knowledge of Walloon and Hebrew, and Welsh although he never preached in it.

- Throughout his life he was noted for displaying a strong interest in the education of children. Barely a day went past without him visiting the National School in Brecon Road, and not just to teach scripture, as the complimentary inspection report of 1847 testified.
- As vicar to the Hay Union Workhouse near St Mary's Church, he championed the education of the pauper children. At his insistence they were admitted to the National School, which was just behind the Workhouse, in 1861. This was years before the compulsory education act and in the teeth of strong opposition from those who believed mixing the children would lead to an improvement in the workhouse children to the detriment of the other pupils. In this they were very mistaken. Once the existing poor standards at the school were improved all pupils benefitted equally.
- A strong supporter of the value of education, he was a member of the Breconshire Education Committee.
- In an educational role, he gave lectures, such as 'The Electric Telegraph' given on 12 November 1856 in the Town Hall in Broad Street.
- His interest in education does not account for why in the 1851 census Augustus Harnet, a pupil born in 1836 at Tours in France, appears as a member of the household. Children left school at far earlier ages than 15 years so perhaps this was some form of religious instruction.
- On 4 August 1866, the Hereford Journal reported on the annual treat hosted by Rev. W.L. Bevan for children of the Hay National School. 'About 170 children were regaled with tea and plum cake'. There were various songs including 'Always Happy', 'O, come ye into the summer woods', 'The Blue Bells of Scotland', 'Whilst I am at school my Father is working on the Farm', 'Hurrah, hurrah for England' and 'God save the Queen'. The girls then played games on the lawn and the boys were taken to Swan Field to play cricket.

Geography was his special interest and his school geography books included:

- A Manual of Geographical Science: Ancient Geography (1859).
- A Students Manual of Modern Geography, Mathematical, Physical and Descriptive. (1868). This was translated into Italian and Japanese.
- The Students Manual of Ancient Geography. Albemarle St London, John Murray (1872).
- Editor, Dr Smith's Smaller Ancient Geography (1872).
- A Manual of Ancient Geography: For the Use of Schools. US Edition.
- Hereford Mappa Mundi, with Canon H.W. Philpott.

After 56 years of stability, the longest-serving resident of the castle moved to Brecon.

Ann Boleyn's Whistle Brooch.

An heirloom still belonging to the descendants of the Bevan family is a small gold brooch now in the Victoria and Albert Museum in London. This exquisite masterpiece dated to *c*1520 is both a brooch and a whistle. It also has three toilet tools, a toothpick, a curved nail pick and an ear wax spoon, folded into the underside of the barrel. On the butt of the handle is engraved the pattern of a snake. Legend has it that it was given to Ann Boleyn by King Henry VIII *c* 1533.

It is typical of the small objects crafted to be sewn onto the robes of rich courtiers and the king himself. This is a rare survivor.

On the scaffold, Ann is said to have given the brooch to a Royal Guard, Captain Gwynn of Swansea for the kindness he had shown her, with the words 'It has a snake upon it and it was a snake who gave it me'. The lieutenant in charge of the Tower at the time was Kyngston, and no Gwynn appears in the records. It is presumed he was a junior officer, perhaps in a dual role of attendant and warder.

The brooch passed down through the guard's family eventually ending up with Richard Gwynn *c*.1750. It then passed to his sister; her son George Jones; his sister Mrs Phillips; and then to her daughter Miss Phillips of Rutland Place, Swansea. In turn, she passed it to her great-nephew, Archdeacon Bevan.[1]

He gave an accurate description of the whistle to Agnes Strickland after she published her book on Ann Boleyn in the 1840s, correcting an assumption she had made about it.[2]

The archdeacon's eldest daughter Mary inherited the brooch, and it has continued to be passed down through the family, although it has now been deposited in the Victoria and Albert Museum. When this occurred is uncertain as it was certainly at the castle on 19 July 1899 when members of the Woolhope Club visited and inspected it.

Chapter 4 - The Golden Age – People.

In 1902 the **Rev. James Allen Smith** succeeded Rev. Bevan but he only lived at the castle for two years before becoming Dean of St David's. His successor **Rev. John Jefferies de Winton** decided that he did not want to use the castle as his home, so he moved the vicarage into Broad Street, and the castle became vacant.

On 17 October 1903, The Field carried a picture of the castle and an advertisement for its unfurnished letting at £200 pa. The accommodation was described as four reception rooms and a large hall, eleven bedrooms, a bathroom with hot and cold, stabling, outbuildings, and a tennis lawn. There was also 'oak panelling permitting of considerable rearrangement'.

The sporting aspect featured prominently with the offer of shooting over 1000 acres, described as mixed but principally partridge. Fishing was not neglected with two miles of the river Wye for trout and several salmon stretches.

The advert offered immediate possession, but it was not until approximately one year later that the castle was successfully leased out by Baron Glanusk.

Lieutenant Colonel A.E. Morrell.

The new tenant was Lt Col Morrell of Priory Terrace, Leamington, who leased the castle in 1904. In reporting this the papers also managed to report his surname as Morrall, an error they committed on numerous other occasions.

As a retired military man, he would have been viewed as being of the right 'calibre' socially to inhabit the castle by the elders of the town. From his point of view the sporting rights, particularly the salmon fishing, may well have been a significant factor in his decision to rent the castle.

In 1905 while the colonel was in residence scaffolding was erected in Castle Street to repair a chimney. A visitor went into Henry Grants the stationers in Castle Street, to buy a postcard of the castle. Henry told him the castle was hundreds of years old. The postcard was duly posted with the following comment on the back 'This is a view of Hay Castle. The man who sold me this card said that the building was hundreds of years old. He's a liar. I have just seen the builders finishing it today'.[3]

Meet of Hounds, Town Clock, Hay

On 17 March 1906 the Colonel hosted the first ever meet in Hay
of the Radnorshire and West Herefordshire Hunt.
A postcard by H.R. Grant, stationer, and photographer of Hay.

Unfortunately for Colonel Morrell his landlord Joseph Russell Bailey, 1st Baron Glanusk, died in 1906. This meant that Dowager Lady Glanusk needed to move out of the family seat, Glanusk Park, to make way for her son the 2nd Baron.

She chose to relocate to Hay Castle, and so after only two years Colonel Morrell was asked to vacate. Leaving it meant that the Morrells had to downsize, as Mr George Perry Price (of Talgarth) announced:

*'honoured with instructions from Lieut-Col Morrall
who is leaving the neighbourhood
to Sell by Auction on Thursday, September 4, 1906,
a portion of the household furniture….'.
This included furniture from virtually every room, a bay brougham horse, harness, a light Landau and various other items.*[4]

Despite the advertisement, it appears that the Colonel was keen not to move too far as he was living at Halidon, Abergavenny, in 1909 when his son Percy was married. The Morrells continued to maintain contact at the castle, and they stayed with Lady Glanusk in May 1919.

Such was the status of association with the castle the local paper reported any items connected to it. Like many families in the country, particularly with military connections, the Morrell family suffered a bereavement during the Great War. Their son Captain Percy was killed in 1917. In making the announcement the paper noted that Lt Col and Mrs Morrell had previously lived at Hay Castle.[5]

Another connection occurred when the papers announced the death of Mrs Mercy Davies (nee Harms) 49 years, wife of Roderick Davies, on 16 May 1919. The obituary noted she was a former maid of Col and Mrs Morrell at Hay Castle. That would have been 11 years earlier.

The Morells must have moved back to Hay as 17 years after they originally left an advert appeared in 1923 for a 'good plain cook aged about 30 years apply Mrs Morrell Wyecliffe, Hay'.

The advertisement described the household consisting of a family of two, this would have been the Col and Mrs Morrell, plus four servants. Wyecliffe is above the river on the opposite side to the Warren to Hay.[6] Col. Morrell was a vice president of the Hay Golf Club for several years up until 1929.

Dowager Lady Glanusk.

The arrival of Mary (Anne Jane, nee Lucas), the Dowager Lady Glanusk at the castle in 1906 marked the beginning of a golden age for it. The comings and goings at the castle were a constant source of local news for the newspapers and the Brecon County Times in particular.

The Dowager, daughter of the eminent local physician Dr Henry Lucas, was born in Crickhowell. She married Sir Joseph Russell Bailey on 9 April 1861. He succeeded his grandfather to become the 2nd Baronet in 1858 and was made 1st Baron Glanusk in 1899. Sadly he died aged only 66 years in January 1906 while opening Brecon War Memorial Hospital.

The couple had a large family of eleven children, of whom nine survived into adulthood. They were all known as The Honourable.

- **(Elizabeth) Mabel Bailey (1862-1952).**

Mabel, born in Llangattock, moved into the castle at the same time as her mother. In 1924 the Brecon County Times summed her up: a Justice of the Peace, well known in district and county organisations for the relief of suffering, particularly nursing organisations, a leader in music circles, and co-opted member of the Board of Guardians at the Hay Workhouse. She was also the president of the Hay Women's Conservative and Unionist Association.

- **Joseph Henry Russell Bailey (1865-1928).**

Joseph joined the Grenadier Guards and served in South Africa in the City of London Imperial Volunteers. On retiring in 1903 he was appointed Lt Col of the 3rd Battalion South Wales Borderers Volunteer Force. On the death of his father, Joseph inherited the title 2nd Lord Glanusk and took up residence at Glanusk Park, the family seat in Crickhowell, in 1906. This is the time that the Dowager moved to Hay.

Joseph's second son Gerald Sergison Bailey 2nd Battalion Grenadier Guards died on 10 August 1915 in the Pas de Calais. His youngest son Midshipman Bernard Michael Bailey was killed at the battle of Jutland.

Joseph's death at only 63 years on 11 January 1928 must have been another devastating blow for his mother. Her sole living grandson Major the Hon. Wilfred Russell Bailey DSO became the 3rd Lord Glanusk. Wilfred visited the castle on 19 September 1919, but it is reasonable to assume he would have been there on numerous other occasions. Joseph's daughter (Dulsie) Editha was a frequent visitor who came to stay with her grandmother.

- **Edith (1866-1933).**

Edith was the only one of the Dowager's daughters to marry. She seems to have caused a family scandal by marrying Samuel Hood Cowper-Coles, an ex-military man, in 1892. On retiring Samuel became a surveyor but was made bankrupt in 1912. Subsequently he became an estate manager and the couple moved to Lower Bisterne, Ringwood, Hampshire. Samuel does not appear to have been welcome at the castle and his wife always seemed to have visited her mother without him.

- **William Bailey (1867-1942).**

William was another military man. He served in the Indian Frontier Expedition during the Tirah Campaign of 1897-8 in the Khyber Pass area of India. In 1916 during the First World War he commanded the 1/1st Welsh Guards. That same year he retired, retaining his rank of major as a reserve officer in the 11th Hussars.

A frequent visitor to the castle, he was a Justice of the Peace and Deputy Lieutenant of Breconshire. One of his retirement hobbies was making rugs and these appeared as prizes at fetes or jumble sales in Hay.[7]

- **Arthur Bailey (1869-1929).**

Arthur was the Dowager's 3rd son and again a military man. He was an officer in the East African Mounted Rifles and served in the Boer War, retiring as a captain. After a spell in Nigeria from 1903-6 he returned to the UK.

Arthur married Miss Elizabeth Ledger Hill of Bulford Manor Wiltshire on 1 July 1924 at St Jude's Church, Courtfield Gardens, South Kensington. The best man was H.H. Prince 'Freddy' Dileep Singh, a regular visitor to the castle. One of the officiating clergymen was his distant cousin the Right Rev. Edward Latham Bevan, Lord Bishop of Swansea and Brecon and the son of Rev. Bevan. He had been brought up at Hay Castle. The reception was at Baileys Hotel, Courtfield Gardens, with the honeymoon in Costello, County Galway.

At the time of his death on 19 January 1929[8] Arthur was living at Oaker Ashton on Clun, Salop. His obituary referred to him as formerly of Hay Castle.

- **Herbert Crawshaw Bailey (1871-1936).**

Herbert went to Oxford University and subsequently was admitted to the Inner Temple in 1897 as a barrister. He had a successful career including being appointed High Commissioner Board of Control in 1924, and later Inspector General of Hospitals. On retirement he became a Justice of the Peace for Middlesex.

On 23 April 1908, he married Kathleen Mary Salt the daughter of Sir Shirley Harris Salt. His son David Russel Bailey became the 4th Baron Glanusk.

- **Margaret Elinor Bailey (1873-1960).**

Margaret never married and became a Deaconess in the Church of England. She devoted herself to religious life and travelled abroad on missionary work. In 1911 she travelled to Bombay on the P&O steamer Mantua.

Lady Glanusk supported the House of Mercy in Swansea, a home for 'fallen women'. It was run by nuns and the inference is that Margaret was associated with it. She returned to stay with her mother on frequent occasions.

- **Gwladys Mary Bailey (b.1875).**

Gwladys, like Mabel, was born in Llangattock and moved permanently to the castle with her mother and sister. A supporter of charitable causes as well as a Justice of the Peace she does not seem to have been as active socially as her sister Mabel, although she was a member of the Boarding House Committee of the Weobley Board of Guardians. After her mother died, she moved to Tretower House, Glanusk Park.

Three years earlier, in 1932, she had advertised for a cook-general for a bachelor's house in Crickhowell, 'where manservant kept and help given'. Age not under 30 years. Who the bachelor was is uncertain but possibly her brother William.

- **John Launcelot Bailey (1879-1918).**

John was the youngest son of Lady Glanusk. In 1903 he married Vivian Dory Carey of Guernsey and moved there to intensively cultivate produce for the early markets.

At the outbreak of war, he responded to his brother Colonel Lord Glanusk's call to volunteer and joined the Brecknock Battalion, South Wales Borders. The battalion sailed for Aden and then on to India where they remained for most of the war. Captain Launcelot Bailey died of influenza at Mhow Central India on 26 October 1918.

Gwladys had a reputation as something of a poet. In 1914 she wrote:

BRECONSHIRE MEN

Harry of Monmouth at Agincourt fought,
His was the life that the enemy sought;
But, in the thick of the fighting, a ring
Of Breconshire soldiers defending the King.
"Over our bodies your way lies" they said
"You cannot touch him until we are dead"
David Gam, Roger Vaughan, Watkin Lloyd
These were then The Breconshire Men.

Now once again, does our army advance
The flower of our manhood is fighting in France:
Again, in the midst of the battle's fierce din,
Breconshire soldiers have died for their King.
More men are wanted – our work is not done,
From Brecon, Crickhowell and Cefn they come;
From Talgarth, Tretower, Ystradgynlais, Brynmawr,
Breconshire men are all ready for war.

Gladly they do it – to answer the call
Of their King and their Fatherland – Patriots all.
King George shall find now as Harry did then,
No soldiers more willing than Breconshire men.
Not for one moment in valour they yield,
To those who fell fighting on Agincourt's field.
Loyal and gallant, and faithful as then are Breconshire men.

The Early Years.

The first ten years of Lady Glanusk's residence in Hay were her most active. In 1910 she commissioned William Douglas Caroe, the renowned architect, to undertake refurbishment and repairs to the mansion. Known mostly for his work on ecclesiastical buildings he altered the internal layout. Unfortunately, there are no extant plans for his alterations.

The castle was the subject of an article in Country Life in September 1914. Very few internal pictures were published and there was little mention of the changes Caroe had made. The article showed the floor plan, with pictures of the Jacobean staircase, and a hall screen which was one of Caroe's changes.

The beautiful plasterwork over a bedroom fireplace[9] may not have been one of Caroe's changes.

In December 1915 the most violent storm in years caused considerable damage in the town. It blew off part of the castle roof, then undergoing repairs, as well as uprooted several trees.

Visitors.

During Lady Glanusk's time, the castle became a Bailey family social hub, with a constant stream of visitors and distinguished guests. Those we know about include:

- **Sir Charles Prestwood Lucas K.C.B., K.C.M.G. (1853 - 1931).**

Lady Glanusk's brother was a frequent guest. Charles gained scholarships to Winchester and Balliol College, where he obtained a first-class degree in classics and humanities. He joined the Colonial Office and retired in 1911 as Assistant Under Secretary of State and Head of the Dominions Department.

Charles never married and lived at St George's Square London with two unmarried sisters. He came to Hay in 1915, twice in 1917 and 1919, and no doubt there were many more occasions.

A visit in 1913 coincided with that of the Bishop of Ely.[10] On this occasion he gave a talk in the Drill Hall entitled 'A tour of Australia' from which he had just returned. On his subsequent visits, he frequently gave such talks in the town.

In retirement, he became principal of the prestigious Working Men's College in St Pancras from 1912 – 22, an institution he had been associated with since 1881.

A keen historian of British colonial development Charles was chairman of the Imperial Studies Committee of the Royal Colonial Institute in 1924. He is buried in Crickhowell.[11]

- **Prince Frederick Victor Dileep Singh.**

On 23 January 1913 'Prince Freddy' as he was known was a guest.[12] He was the son of Sir Dileep Singh the last Maharaja of the Sikh Empire in Punjab, India. The Maharaja was forced to abdicate at the age of 12 years and give the Koh-I-Noor Diamond, now in the crown jewels, to Lord Dalhousie and the British crown. Subsequently he lived in Britain.

Prince Freddy was born in England and educated at Eton and Cambridge. He became an integral member of London society. As a staunch royalist, he kept a portrait of Oliver Cromwell hung upside down in the toilet of his house in Norfolk.

The visit in 1913 was one of a number and may have coincided with home visits by the Hon. Arthur, for whom Prince Freddy acted as best man at his wedding in 1924.

- **Sophia Alexandrovna Dileep Singh (1876-1948).**

Sophia was the sister of Prince Freddy. Although born in Belgravia she was an Indian Princess and a godchild of Queen Victoria. An ardent suffragette she used her influence, and money, to support the cause both in the United Kingdom and India.[13]

Sophia supported the 'No Taxation Without Representation' movement, founded in 1909, and refused to pay her taxes. For this, her assets, including a diamond ring, were confiscated and auctioned off. As she was also a founder member of the Women's Taxation Resistance League (1909-18) the members of the league bought all her possessions and returned them to her.

In 1934, long after women's representation had been achieved, she visited the castle.

- **Emily Agnes Liddell (1867-1934).**

The Hon. Emily was a visitor to the castle in 1921. She was single and may have been a friend of either Mabel, who was six years older, or Gwladys, who was seven years younger. Her father Arthur Thomas Liddell was a clerk in the War Office until he was 57 years old. On the death of his cousin Athole Charles John Liddell, he then became the 5th Baron Ravensworth. Emily's mother Sophia Harriett was born in Belgium, the daughter of Sir Thomas Waller, Bart.

Emily's extended family included Alice, and her sisters Edith and Lorina. They became the inspiration for Charles Dodgson to write, as Lewis Carroll, the Alice in Wonderland stories.

Fishing.

From 1845, and the arrival of the archdeacon, the inhabitants of the town had access to fishing in the river Wye from the bridge to the Dulas Brook. This was confirmed by Lord Glanusk in 1907. Hay Town Council wrote to the Glanusk Estate in 1925 requesting that the town's fishing rights be extended in the opposite direction from Hay Bridge to Loggin Brook. An agent for Major the Hon. Wilfred Bailey, Lord Glanusk, acknowledged the request but said that this was stated as included in the lease of the castle. He 'regretted the matter could not be entertained'.[14]

With the castle having rights over its own waters fishing understandably was popular with members of the family and guests. The Hay Castle Game Register records the first entries in 1906, the year Lady Glanusk arrived. Any chance to mention salmon fishing was also seized on by the press. The fishing was also an excuse, or a lure, to invite notable visitors.

The Brecon County Times reported in March 1914 that Maj. the Hon William Bailey caught two salmon, 23.5lb. and 17.5lb., despite the Rivers Usk and Hondu running high and being full of snow at Brecon.[15]

The following month William was accompanied by Lieutenant Sir R.S.S. Baden-Powell, author of Scouting for Boys when they went fishing in Hay Castle waters.[16] Akala Miss Tunnard-Moore took the opportunity to ensure that Baden-Powell met her local scout troop.

Local 'worthies' also made use of the fishing opportunities. In 1925 the Hay Castle Game Register recorded:

> *'On Tuesday March 31 D. Powell fishing Steeple Poole with floating prawn lost a fish, and tackle. On Wed he and Major Booth went down again and saw the float, then D. cast over it, and fouled it, the fish was still on and was finally landed 22lbs.'*

Participating members of the Bailey family included Arthur, Gerald, William, Mabel, Herbert and (John) Lancelot. The dowager also permitted locals to use the castle waters: E. Tunnard-Moore (originally from Frampton Hall, Lincolnshire but by now at Cusop), Major Cockcroft, E. and M. Butler, and Lt. Colonel Richard Garnons Williams. His younger brother Royal Navy Fleet Surgeon Commander Penry Garnons Williams was also a member of a fishing party.

Three 'names' in the register were to lose their lives in the oncoming war:
- Lancelot Bailey died of influenza at Mhow in 1918.
- Richard Garnons Williams was killed on the battlefield at Loos in September 1915.
- Penry Garnons Williams was lost with Lord Kitchener when HMS Devonshire was sunk off the Orkney Islands when she was on the way to Russia in 1917.

Date.	Beat.	Guns.	Rabbits.	Hares.	Pheasants.	Grouse.	Partridges.	Woodcock.
		Bt forward.						
May 5	Middle Warren	A Bailey						
" 6th	Rock Pool	Gerald Bailey						
14	Lapstone	E. Trinnard Moore						
15	Bottom stream	E. Trinnard Moore						
19"	Rock Pool	Gerald Bailey						
20th	Lower Stream	W. Bailey						
21	Bottom Stream	E. Trinnard Moore						
June 13	Lapstone	M Bailey						
Aug 29	Sheep house	HCB. JLB.	2	–	–		–	–
Sept 2nd	Sheep house	HCB JLB. MB	2	–	–	–	15	–
5th	do	do	2	–	–	–	16	–
20	do	Mr Cockcroft, E. J. Hughes	2	–	–	–	17	–
Oct 2nd	do	HCB. MB	1	–	17	–	4	–
Oct. 11	Lower stream	Mr Both						
13	– – –	– – –						
Nov. 6	On hill	N. B. R. G. Williams, E. Butler	2		1			1
Nov. 24	Sheep house	Cd: Gurney Williams, Mr Butler	1		12		2	
			12		30		54	1

The May to November entries in the Hay Castle Fish and Game record for 1913 (1).

Hay Castle Fish and Game record (2).

The opposite page in the register gives the size of the individual salmon with the flies they were caught on, with the reliable 'Dusty Miller' catching the largest specimen. The 30 trout do not even warrant mention of their combined weight. The shooting record for Sheephouse, just outside Hay, and shown on the lower half of the page, include rabbits, pheasants, partridge, a solitary woodcock, snipe, and pigeons.

Indoor Female Servants.

With such a relatively large house, and a constant stream of visitors, servants at the castle were essential.

In 1911 the servants who lived in were Christina Mary Cottrell cook, Florence Lewis maid, housemaids Florence Ada Morgan and Ellen Elsie Ballinger, and Jane Davies kitchen maid. None of the servants were born in Hay. By 1921 there was an additional housemaid.

There seems to have been a constant demand for new staff. Multiple post-war adverts appeared:

- 3 Sept.1919 – Kitchen maid. Wanted in a small family. Address to Dowager Lady Glanusk…[17]
- 24 July 1920 - Wanted. A Head Housemaid where two are kept.[18]
- 15 November 1923 - Wanted kitchen maid.[19]
- 2 October 1924 - Wanted kitchen maid.[20]
- 6 November 1924 - Wanted a Parlourmaid.[21]
- 9 July 1925 - Wanted an under-Housemaid.[22]
- 5 December 1924 – Parlourmaid wanted who understands silver.[23]
- 26 September 1926 - Upper housemaid where two are kept.[24]
- 17 Sept 1930 - Cook – kitchen maid kept.[25]
- 2 April 1931 – Wanted strong girl required as kitchen maid.[26]
- 3 June 1931 - Wanted strong girl required as kitchen maid.[27]
- 7 September 1933 – Wanted kitchen maid.[28]
- 19 October 1933 - Wanted a Parlourmaid.[29]

Outdoor Male Servants.

Joseph H. Davies was described as a former coachman at his funeral in November 1914.[30] This was a few years after Lady Glanusk sold her Brougham, small brake and a set of double harness when she acquired a car so this may have been the time he retired.

Steven Lewis Turner was chauffeur to Lady Glanusk when he married Ethel May Evans on 28 February 1912 in Hay. He received cheques from the Dowager, Mabel, Gwladys and Major William as wedding presents.

Gardener.

The castle always had a gardener. John Jones from Middleton-on-the-Hill in Herefordshire took up the post of Head Gardener sometime between 1910-14. He lived at Clyro with his wife Edith and their six children.

Their 15-year-old daughter Mary, a teacher at the church Sunday school, died in December 1916. Mabel, Gwladys and staff from the castle attended the funeral.[31] John's wife Edith died, aged 40, on 24 October 1918, possibly from the Spanish Flu. This left John with five young children.[32]

John worked 8 am to 5 pm Monday to Friday. On Saturdays, he would take his youngest sons Albert and Lennie with him to water the vegetables. Sometimes Lady Glanusk would catch Alfred eating the strawberries. After asking his father's permission she would take him back to the castle where Bramwell the Hall Porter escorted Alfred to the kitchen. There Miss Clarke the cook would open the biscuit tin and give him a glass of milk. All the staff knew he had lost his mother.

To help John in his job Lady Glanusk would permit her chauffeur to take him to Glanusk Park on a Sunday. There he would confer with the head gardener, exchange plants and flowers and discuss gardening matters.

John earned £3 a week and at Christmas he was given a ton of coal and a new suit. John would then negotiate with a clothier in Castle Street for his children to be provided with new clothes of the same value, instead of the new suit.

In February 1916 John was mentioned in connection with an incident when Josiah Greenway, 12 years old, damaged trees in the grounds of the castle. For this Josiah was fined 10s and bound over.[33] Josiah appears to have been something of a tearaway as later his father was fined £2 because Josiah broke into his grandfather's house and stole £12 10s. His two older accomplices went to prison for one month.

Lady Glanusk always made sure that poor families in the town received surplus produce from the castle gardens, such as cabbage, lettuce and peas. If someone was ill, or there was a bereavement, John would be asked to take cut flowers to the family.

John Jones Head Gardener and Mrs (Edith Adelaide?) Madigan.
Photograph courtesy of Martin Hewitt.

Indoor Male Servants.

Only one male servant was employed indoors at the castle, and he was confined to the ground floor. In 1911 John James Brooks was a footman. When he moved on in early 1919 an advertisement for his replacement appeared. 'Lad Wanted, between 15 and 16, to help in the house and in the garden; to live in – Apply Dowager Lady Glanusk, Hay Castle.'[34]

Daniel Cornish was appointed, and he quickly obtained advancement to the post of Hall Boy. He only stayed for two years, so a further similar advertisement appeared on 15 September 1921. Edward Young was then appointed. He was older, and as far as the town was concerned, he was referred to as the butler, possibly a previous position he held. Edward retired in 1928 and died in 1931. On Edward's retirement, another advertisement for a kitchen boy appeared and Emma Lloyd decided this was a golden opportunity for her grandson Bramwell.

Bramwell Bradley.

Bramwell's grandmother Emma was born in New Tredegar Monmouthshire and came to Hay in 1890 as a lieutenant in the Salvation Army. She met her husband Evan Lloyd, a stonemason from Glasbury, when he went along to an army meeting at the Wheatsheaf Inn in Lion Street intent on causing disruption. Instead, he fell in love with Emma and they married in 1892.

Bramwell's mother Maud Elizabeth Lloyd was born in the autumn of 1894. She married Harold Bradley in Hay in the summer of 1912. Harold was a Great Western Railways platelayer living at 9 Abergarw Road, Brynmawr, Bridgend, in 1911.

By 1916 he was registered no. 743078 in the National Union of Railwaymen, Barry 1, Glamorgan, and he still retained that job at the time of his death. On 24 Sept 1918, aged 23 years, he was hit and killed by a train in Cardiff while walking home with a sack of potatoes on his back.

Bramwell's grandmother Emma remembers seeing Harold in his coffin. He was pink, felt warm to the touch and his flesh bounced back, unlike other family members Emma visited to pay her respects to in later life. As she got older she was haunted by the thought that Harold may have been in a deep coma and was buried alive.

Emma thought that in the early 19th century the doctors may not have detected a faint heartbeat. She always had her children and grandchildren promise to put a mirror under her nose to make sure she was dead before she was buried.[35]

Bramwell was born in July 1913. He went to live with his grandparents Emma and Evan when his mother married soldier George Williams on 25 September 1920. The Lloyds lived in Bear Street, Hay. By this time their two eldest children had left home. Their youngest son Herbert aged 11 was still at school when Bramwell joined the family. Bramwell was never formally adopted.

Bramwell left school at 14 years of age and went to work for chemist Fred Davies. It was only a year later a friend of his grandmother pointed out that a vacancy had been advertised for a houseboy at the castle.[36] At his grandmother's urging Bramwell quickly applied. Wednesday was his half day, so an interview was arranged for that afternoon. This meant he did not have to resign from his current job at the chemist to go to the interview.

At the end of his interview Lady Glanusk was sufficiently impressed to offer him the job, for which he was required to make a decision that afternoon. He agreed, at a sum of 12s 6d per week, payable monthly, together with room and board. This was a major increase from the 7s 6d paid by Fred Davies. His grandmother was so pleased, her grandson working at the castle!

Bramwell's hours of work were from 6.30 am to 11.30 pm daily and his training followed the 'castle system'. For the first six months he worked in the kitchen, as well as doing various odd jobs and helping out in the garden. After that, he graduated to more responsible house duties as a footman and reduced his help in the garden. Because he quickly proved himself, and he was promoted to become the Hall Porter.

Effectively Bramwell became the butler but could not officially be called that because there was no footman. Such was the etiquette of the time. To the town, he was the butler. Bramwell stayed for seven years, and we have an account of his time at the castle detailing the daily routine and his duties. This includes a record of visitors of note. As a discrete servant, Bramwell did not name them, but many are easy to identify and have been included in this history.

In the summer, when the family were away, he gave tours of the castle. In addition to the history of the building, Bramwell liked to tell stories. A mark on the stairs in the brown hall became a bloodstain from a gruesome murder, with the outline of the keys the housekeeper dropped when she discovered the body still indelibly imprinted in it. A ghostly monk 'with piercing eyes and pointy shoes' roamed the corridors at night, and a secret tunnel went under the castle and the river Wye all the way to Clifford Castle, three miles away.

Another story he liked to relate was when a lady's maid came screaming down the stairs.
    'Bramwell, Bramwell, there is a rat in Lady Glanusk's bath'.
    'What do you expect me to do about it?'
    'You are the man of the house, deal with it.'
On checking sure enough there was a rat sitting on the tray over the bath eating the soap. What to do? He had an idea. Scuttling down to the kitchen he grabbed the fire poker. Returning to the bathroom the rat was duly knocked off and drowned in the bath.

Now what? Running downstairs again to collect the fire tongs, these proved the ideal tool to remove the rat and throw it out of the window. As it was the end of his shift he went off duty. The question is, did Lady Glanusk have a bath in the water the rat drowned in? In practice, it was probably a mouse but a rat makes a better story, and Bramwell liked to tell stories.

Another story about Bramwell shows his mischievous character. There were railings by the castle gates and children used to swing on them. This despite being told not to as Bramwell wouldn't like it and would frighten them. Ignoring this advice they were playing by the gates one evening as it was getting dark when suddenly the gates opened. Coming down the drive was a ghostly white apparition – a pair of legs with a sheet over its head! It was Bramwell.[37]

After Lady Glanusk died in 1935 Bramwell locked the castle for the final time and left Hay. He eventually ended up in Birmingham. In 1939 he was living at 2 Trysull Avenue and employed as a petrol pump attendant. Later that year he married Phoebe Edith Parton, born in 1914, at Wednesbury.

After the war Bramwell qualified as a chiropodist. When Phoebe died in 1978 he was ordained a bishop in the Reformed Catholic Church. This broke away from the church in Rome in 1870. While it celebrates the same sacraments and liturgy the church follows a more liberal progressive path, such as the ordination of men and women and affirming the LGBTQ community. He continued to live in Birmingham.

Bramwell William Arthur Bradley died on 5 December 2007 aged 94, two days after having a leg amputated under local anaesthetic.

Secret Tunnel.

Bramwell liked to talk about a secret tunnel to Clifford, no evidence of which was known at the castle at the time. This changed in 1993 when a long-time resident of Hay, Mary Edwards, gave an interview. Her story about a tunnel was published in HayWire the local, somewhat scurrilous, news sheet.

Mary said her husband Tom Evans was working in the grounds of the castle when the ground subsided and he fell into a hole. It was so deep he could not climb out and had to shout for help to get someone to come to rescue him. Tom and several other men then collected torches and a couple of canaries and went back into the hole to follow a brick, or stone, lined tunnel until they came to a brick wall.

From this incident various stories emerged, possibly embellished by mischievous locals such as Cyril Marwood the journalist and Freddy Stokoe a long-time resident of Hay e.g., the canaries died, the tunnel extended under Hay Cheesemarket, and was the scene of 'Fair Rosamund's' murder. None of the stories can be substantiated of course, but who knows what in time may be discovered under the castle lawns!

Chapter 5 - The Golden Age – Events.

Supporting the War Effort.

The castle galvanised all its recourses to support the war effort as best it could. Lady Glanusk was President of the Hay Needlework Society, which supported the Red Cross and the Soldiers & Sailors Families Association.[1]

As early as August 1914 the castle hosted a meeting to arrange sewing classes to make garments for soldiers.[2] In November Mabel issued an appeal for warm woollen garments for her brother (Major William Bailey) and other members of the Welsh Horse Regiment stationed in Norfolk before they were due to go to the continent.[3]

The same month Lady Glanusk's granddaughter Editha Glanusk started an appeal for £25 to make plum puddings to be sent to 'our gallant Territorials'. The family responded by the Dowager donating £1, Lady Glanusk at Glanusk Park, (Editha's mother) donating two guineas (£2.2s) and Mabel also contributed. Two years later she made another appeal this time for vegetables, eggs, rabbits, and fish to send to the War Hospital at Brecon to feed the wounded troops who had been evacuated home from 'the great advance'.[4] This would have been the Somme.

The Brecknock Battalion South Wales Borderers was sent to Aden at the start of the war. Many local men served in the battalion. In June 1915 Archdeacon Edward Latham Bevan vicar of Brecon gave a talk about 'Life in Aden' where he had been to support the Welsh troops. Edward was a son of the previous occupant of the castle Archdeacon William Latham Bevan, a cousin of the family, and well-known in the town.[5]

In January 1915 the War Relief Work Society met at the castle. They decided to make clothes for Belgian soldiers interned in Holland.[6] In August Mabel started a subscription to send shaving and hair-cutting requisites for the 16 men of the South Wales Borderers now prisoners of war in Germany. £4 was contributed immediately.[7]

In December 1915 Mabel had a letter published appealing for support for Lady Kensington's appeal for 'Comforts for the Welsh Horse' serving at Anzac in the Dardanelles.[8]

Staff at Hay Castle sent a Christmas card in 1915 to 'Our 'Boy from the Old Folks at Home'. Photograph taken on the castle lawn. Mabel Bailey is in the back row first on the left.

Lady Glanusk was in constant demand to open fetes, fairs and charitable events. On Thursday 16 December 1915 she opened a 'jumble sale' for the Glasbury Branch of the Farmers Union held at the Clock Tower, Hay. Proceeds from the sale of the auctioned live and dead farm stock, poultry, fruit, etc were to be divided between local Breconshire and Radnorshire hospitals for the war wounded and the National Fund for the Comforts of Welsh Troops.[9]

Red Cross.

Particularly during the war, the castle always gave support to the Red Cross when it could. Before the war, however, the St John's Ambulance Association had a major presence there. In February 1913 medallions, vouchers and certificates were handed out to the successful candidates in the First Aid and Home Nursing classes.[10]

The organiser of the classes was the redoubtable Miss Anna Tunnard-Moore and the group presented her with a hand bag for first aid supplies in recognition of her efforts on their behalf.

Mrs J.J. de Winton the vicar's wife made the presentations and on presenting the hand bag read out a ditty composed by the Hon. Mabel Bailey.

> Our dear Miss Anna Tunnard-Moore, -
> All your friends here feel very sure,
> That if it had not been for you
> They would not ever have got through
> Their difficult examination.
> ……..
> And should there ever come a day
> When Suffragettes should invade Hay,
> Frighten the policemen off their beat,
> Shop windows smash in Castle Street,
> And shoot and scratch, and tear and bite
> The men who dare to show some fight
> Then – led by you – we all will tend,
> And greatly sooth each wounded friend
> (For shame it is those fiends should vex,
> And roughly treat the other sex.)

Who said Hay was gentile backwater oblivious of national events?

A year later in May 1914, before the clouds of war had appeared on the horizon, the castle hosted a meeting to hand out certificates to members of the Red Cross, some of whom were present a year earlier.

At the meeting Lady Glanusk read a saying from St. Augustine.

> *'If God had designed woman to be man's master He would have taken her from his head; if as his slave, He would have taken her from his feet; but as He designed her for his companion and equal, He took her from his side'.*

The Dowager then went on to give her view:

> *'It is a mistake for women to try and do men's work for which they are not fitted, either physically or mentally; they had far better study to fit themselves to be thoroughly efficient women by learning to do more things which they can do better than men, and while men are trained in the art of war, women should perfect themselves amongst other things in the essentially womanly art of nursing….pray God, should the day come when England is threatened with invasion, her sons and daughters may be found shoulder to shoulder and 'ready, aye, ready' to take their parts in working for their King and country.'*[11]

In April 1915 there was a meeting at the castle of the Hay & Cusop Nursing Association.[12] In May 1916 Mabel presented certificates to Red Cross members who had passed their exams.

The castle was too small to be requisitioned as a rehabilitation hospital but in January 1916 Lady Glanusk entertained wounded soldiers from the Red Cross Hospitals at Sarnesfield and Llyswen.[13] Later in August sixty members of the Red Cross attended a meeting at the castle. Commandant Miss Tunnard-Moore reported that 545 garments had been made for service personnel.

Mabel was a benefactor to many causes. This included the Welsh-based Evening Express Prisoners of War fund which sent food parcels to captured members of the Welsh regiment. Lloyd George was the patron and Major James German was the chairman. On the Tuesday Mabel subscribed a total sum of £688 was raised.[14]

In 1921 the balance sheets of the Hay and Cusop Soldiers and Sailors Reception Fund and the Hay and Cusop Memorial Fund were presented.[15] Mabel was the chair of both funds, and she was credited with being the driving force in raising the £264.11s.6d. This was sufficient to pay for the new town war memorial.

Other events.

In August 1916 tea was provided for 30 members of the Mothers Meeting, although what their contribution was to the war effort is not known. Possibly it was an occasion to provide moral support for mothers with boys away at war, or children with fathers absent due to the conflict.[16]

The principal of Coleg Trevecca Mr T. Howat gave an address at the castle on 'Reconstruction after the War' in which he encouraged a spirit of cooperation and service. He thanked Dowager Lady Glanusk and the Hon. Mabel Bailey, perhaps showing the Dowager's increased reliance on her daughter for support.[17]

Once the war was over thoughts moved to the future, and there were discussions on how to celebrate repatriation after the war. Mabel suggested a garden party on the lawn at the castle.[18]

Family Tragedy.

Like most families, the Glanusks were directly affected by the war. In addition to the death of her son Launcelot, two of Lady Glanusk's grandsons died. They were the children of the 2nd Baron, Joseph Henry Russell Bailey and his wife Editha Elma.

Second Lieut. the Hon. Gerald Sergison Bailey 2nd Bn. Grenadier Guards was the second son of Lady Glanusk. After school at Eton and agricultural college at Cirencester Gerald went to Uasin Gishu in British East Africa (now Kenya) as a farmer. At the outbreak of war, he served as a Lieut. in the Kings African Rifles Nairobi Field Force before transferring to the Grenadier Guards.[19] He was killed on 10 August 1915 on the Menin Road, Ypres and is buried in the Guards Cemetery, Windy Corner, Cuinchy.

Mid. Hon. B. M. BAILEY,
H.M.S. Defence.

His brother the Hon. Bernard Michael Bailey died in 1916. He was a midshipman on H.M.S. Defence when she was 'sunk in the recent great naval battle off Jutland'.[20] HMS Defence was under heavy fire from the German battleship Friedrich Der Grosse when she blew up with the loss of all 904 hands.

Gerald and Bernard were the older brothers of Wilfred who became the 3rd Lord Glanusk. They are commemorated on the War Memorial in Hay.

Charitable Support.

When Lady Glanusk was living at Glanusk Park before her husband died her family was heavily involved with the town of Abergavenny. In a typical instance, Gwladys was the 'official for art' at the 1907 Abergavenny 23rd Annual Eisteddfod.[21] However, once Lady Glanusk moved into the castle, she transferred her energies to Hay. She and her daughters quickly integrated into the town and provided support for multiple charities and voluntary organisations.

The castle was the ideal setting for many of these events. Hay had a Skating Rink Group. Where the said rink was, if it was ever built, is unknown, certainly not at the castle. The Wye rarely froze over in winter but perhaps waters were drained off the river into a shallow pond which could freeze. During the summer of 1910, the group held a social event on the castle lawns to play tennis and other games.

In addition to the St. John's Ambulance Association ceremony, in September 1913 entertainment on the castle lawns raised £6.4s. for the Boy Scouts Fund. There was also a pastoral play, 'The Haymakers' where 'Mr. E.H. Cheese the solicitor lent his piano gratis'.[22]

In May the following year the local honourable secretary of the Waifs and Strays Society, Mabel Bailey again, organised a garden meeting. After an address by the Rev. R.J. Keble, a 'Parcel Tea' was organized. If guests chose not to bring a parcel, there was a charge of 1s.[23]

July 1913 saw the Church of England Zenana Missionary Society hold a meeting at the castle.[24] This was an Anglican Missionary Society that worked in India where the purdah system meant women, particularly widows, were segregated in their own quarters known as Zenana. Unrelated men were not allowed to enter. As a result, the women were largely denied healthcare.

The society was set up to support these women. For the first 100 years only women were employed. They were trained as nurses, and some were medically qualified (women were unable to practice as doctors in the UK at this time). As well as providing healthcare support they could spread the Christian message. Lady Glanusk's daughter Margaret was an Anglican Deaconess, and it seems she was a member of the missionary society as she was in Delhi in 1911.

The society has evolved into Interserve a Christian society working to support the neediest people in the Asian and Arab worlds.

The exigencies of war meant that other charitable events at the castle appear to have been reduced. Possibly it was just that war news precluded their reporting. The town held a 'Quiet Day' in July 1916 when services were held in the church, free meals were provided in the National School Brecon Road, and the castle gardens were opened for the day. Support for some favoured organisations included, in July 1917, Gwladys organising the annual meeting of the Girls Friendly Society.[25]

It was in May two years later that 'Lady Glanusk organised' a Punch & Judy show for children at Hay Castle, although it is unlikely she did more than give permission![26] In August 1919 the Abertillery Silver Band played on the lawn of the castle before a great crowd.[27] Use of the lawns for tea parties, hosted by members of the family, were a regular occurrence, such as the Girls Friendly Society tea of 1921.

There is a large hiatus in reported events from then onwards. It seems unlikely that they ceased altogether but perhaps the papers were concentrating on more dynamic news. Mundane events, important to the local community but not of newspaper interest, would have occurred such as local schoolchildren dancing the maypole.

In 1926 The Hay Historic Pageant in ten episodes was produced on the castle grounds with: Interesting Episodes, Gorgeous Dresses, Magnificent Scenes, and Dainty Dances. Sweet and provision stalls, Tea served at reasonable rates. Entrance 1s seats extra.[28]

A poor-quality image but it shows children Maypole dancing on the castle lawns.
Photograph courtesy of Simon Morris.

It was unusual events that sparked a journalistic interest. By October 1928 Lady Dowager was in her 88th year when an unusual musical event was given on the castle lawns. After a performance by the Hay Folk Dancers and child dancers, an illuminated display was given by the St Mary's Hay Brigade of the Church Lads Brigade, led by their captain Mr Rhys Harding. This consisted of torch-light mass marching, electric wand, the march of the toy soldiers, musical callisthenics, and a gymnastic display. The event was completed by the 'Peace Pact Ballet'.[29]

In 1931 Lady Glanusk hosted a free firework display on the 5 November for the children of the town. This was supervised by John Jones the head gardener.

Family Members Support for Charities.

In addition to hosting events themselves, the individual members of the family gave their support to many events and causes held elsewhere. On Wednesday 24 July 1907:

'a Grand Bazaar and Garden Fete was held at Gwernyfed Park, opened by the Lord Bishop of St David's. Stall no. 7, Glass and China was run by Dowager Lady Glanusk, Mrs RD Garnons-Williams wife of Lt Col Richard Garnons-Williams of Cusop and Mrs J.J. de Winton wife of the vicar of Hay. Contributions to any of the stalls in money or in kind were gratefully received by stallholders or by the Hon. Sec. Hon. Mabel Bailey, Hay Castle.'[30]

The bazaar seems to have been an annual event as Mabel was similarly involved as secretary in the bazaar in 1912.

As Lady Glanusk grew older her daughters Mabel and Gwladys became the major forces in supporting charitable events. As an example, they promoted the mystery play Eager Heart in the Parish Rooms in December 1919. A mystery play, in honour of the Nativity of our Lord, was performed at the Parish Hall on 11-13 December 1922 and promoted by Gwladys.[31]

While Gwladys helped her sister it is obvious from the reports that Mabel, possibly as she was the eldest, increasingly became the lead in this charitable work. After the war, as the years progressed, she increasingly took the place of her mother, the Dowager.

Opening community facilities must have been part and parcel of their support for the town. On 1 May 1925 Mabel opened the combined sports ground on Brecon Road. This provided a cricket ground, tennis courts and a bowling green in one location for the Wye Hotel Sports Club. These were in addition to the courts of the Wyeside Tennis Club.[32]

In December 1925 Hay Players performed the Gilbert and Sullivan Operetta HMS Pinafore in the Drill Hall. The paper reported that the excellent standard of the players was attributed to the support provided by Mabel, who conducted the orchestra.[33]

Mabel had already founded the Hay Glee Club a few years earlier. Members gave her a black ebony silver mounted baton in appreciation of her support at the end of the 1922 season.

Some of the events they were called upon to attend seem quite remote from their home territory. In 1933 Mabel presented the prizes to the winners at the Brynmawr Sports Day, 30 miles away.[34]

Both sisters likely took an interest in local history as they subscribed to the Brecknock Society. In 1934 they supported the society's appeal for £1,400 to top up the £1,500 from the Pilgrim Trust to purchase Tretower Court near Crickhowell. The society intended to present the old semi-fortified Breconshire manor house to the nation.[35] It is now under the care of CADW.

The Brecknock Society held its annual general meeting at 6 pm on Saturday 22 July 1933 at the castle to celebrate the completion of work undertaken by the Dowager's late husband. Lord Glanusk had been working on an update of Theophilus Jones famous History of Brecknock before he died. The updated history was in four volumes with volumes I and II published in 1909 and volume III in 1911. The final volume IV was published in 1930, with all four enhanced with notes by Lord Glanusk.

After a sumptuous tea provided 'gratis' by Dowager Lady Glanusk, the society thanked Dr Pringle for his work in completing the 'Glanusk Edition' bringing the history up to date and completing Lord Glanusk's work. In presenting a 'fine bound edition' of the fourth volume to Dr Pringle, Mabel said she was pleased to see that her father's work had now come to fruition.[36]

In a wider Breconshire interest Mabel was involved in work at Brecon Cathedral. In the Archdeaconry of Brecon elections for the seventy or so members of the governing body in 1924 Mabel was elected to the Lay Committee of Group II.[37]

Perhaps it was in this capacity Mabel added her name as the Hon. Sec. Breconshire to a letter appealing for money towards 'rebuilding the worn-out cathedral organ which cannot be delayed' at Brecon Cathedral. The sum to be raised was £2,500. Their aim was for 100 people to contribute £10, 100 to contribute £5 and 1000 to contribute £1.

This appeal was very shortly after the foundation of the new diocese of Swansea and Brecon.[38] The first bishop of the new diocese was her brother Edward. He presented the Bevington Organ his father used to play in the hall of the castle to the cathedral. It is possible that this was used while the main cathedral organ was being rebuilt.

Progress was slow despite the Brecon County Times of 10 March 1927 publishing a list of the great and the good of the county and the amounts they had subscribed. During 1926 and the first part of 1927 they raised £486.2s.3d.

Mabel was also involved in fundraising for Brecon Memorial Hospital. On 'Pound Day' 1932 Mabel's team of collectors in Hay and Llanigon collected cash of £3.1s.3d., four and half doz. eggs, eleven and a half lbs. tea, 325 lbs. groceries and one cucumber.[39]

House of Mercy Swansea.

Lady Glanusk was a prominent supporter of this charitable institution, one of a number in South Wales. The first House of Mercy, for South Wales and Monmouthshire, opened in Cardiff in 1862. It was designed as a place where 'fallen women', i.e. they had 'lost their innocence' by engaging in sexual activities outside marriage, could be re-educated.

By giving them domestic skills, particularly laundry work, they could 'wash away their sins', earn a living and become useful members of society. The homes were strictly run with a rigid routine, including religious instruction. The aim was to create a home for inmates, and the nuns to become substitute mothers to them. It is well established that a number of requests for admittance were to escape abusive or controlling parents.

The House of Mercy in Swansea was run by Anglican nuns, which suggests Lady Glanusk's support for it stemmed from her Deaconess daughter Margaret working there. There has never been any suggestion that they bore any comparison to the Magdalene Laundries in Ireland.

Emeralds.

The castle was the subject of a number of rumours related to the legend of Matilda de Braose's emeralds being hidden in it somewhere. A letter in the Brecon County Times in 1911 referred to a story that a lead casket was found while repairs were being made to the castle wall on Oxford Road. The 'Hayite' suggested that they might be the mythical lost emeralds of 'Moll Walbee'.

The letter cites the legend that King John's Queen Isabella requested them in return for Matilda's liberty from King John's custody.[40] Her reply 'The emeralds are with emerald more beautiful still' has intrigued searchers for years.

The letter continues with another emerald story related to the time the castle was let in sections (i.e. under the Wellingtons). George Psalmanager was said to have been a tenant of the castle and 'the wily fellow' worked out that the gems were hidden in the grounds under the grass. All the work he did in planting trees and shrubs and digging drains, showed he did all he could to find them.[41]

George Psalmanazar 'native of Formosa'. Available under https://creativecommons.org/publicdomain/zero/1.0/.

The stories about George Psalmanazar (1679-1763) are intriguing. He claimed to be the first Formosan (present-day Taiwan) to visit Europe and even claimed to speak the language. In reality, he was a Frenchman probably born in the Languedoc or Provence, although his real name is still a mystery. He claimed to have been raised by the Jesuits but kept all details of his childhood obscure. As a young man, there were years of travel throughout Europe, including employment as a soldier in the Low Countries, before he arrived in London in 1703.

Almost immediately Psalmanager featured widely in scientific and literary circles. He managed to fool everyone with tall tales about the island and the mythical people who inhabited it. After an intense few years of fame, he was eventually unmasked in 1706. Despite this his invented language appeared in lexicons well into the 19th century.[42] He was a friend of Samuel Johnson.

Psalmanazar kept detailed diaries but, despite the rumours, there is no mention of Hay in them or any evidence he visited Hay or ever lived at the castle.[43] Another Hay myth?

Town's Pride.

Hosting so many charitable events and good causes may have contributed to the pride the people in the town felt for the castle and its occupants. They were quick to complain of any perceived slight, and to reinforce their pride in the institution generally.

A correspondent in the Radnor Express in February 1907 deprecated the growing eyesore of telegraph poles spoiling views. As an example, he cited the one adjacent to the stone steps leading up to the ancient gateway of the castle. Even worse in his view were the two china insulators attached to the castle keep. He called attention to 'the need for something being done to preserve the old dear'.[44]

The Town Council were also quick to use the honour of the castle to illustrate a point. At one of its meetings in 1915, the issue of the poor water supply to the town was discussed. The example used was that when the supply was fully switched on there was still not enough pressure to reach the castle.[45]

Two other instances were demonstrated by the Freemason's Lodge. In December 1914 Wor. Bro. H. Graystone gave a large crest to the Lodge in memory of Wor. Bro. C.T. Evans. The work was 'exquisitely carved in oak' by Mr T. Watkins of Market Street. The design represented the portcullis gateway to Hay Castle with the motto 'In Haia Salus'.[46]

A year later the Rev. J.J. de Winton gave a banner depicting Hay Castle to the Hay Lodge, painted by Prof. Van Emelen.[47] The professor was a Belgian refugee who came to Hay in late 1914 with his family of five children. The town supported them by providing accommodation at no. 6 Church Street. In April 1915 Prof. Van Emelen obtained a teaching post at Christ College and the family moved to Brecon.

Newspaper Reports.

Any letter from the family to the press was always published. In 1923 the Brecon County Times carried a letter headed 'Dowager Lady Glanusk's Protest'. Mary Glanusk wrote stating 'a great many people were shocked and distressed at the irreverent and heartless exhibition at the carnival (on Tuesday 13 September 1923). One float featured a mock coffin with a girl dressed in white (as a corpse) and a man purporting to be a clergyman. It seemed particularly heartless when all were feeling the loss of someone who was much loved.'[48]

Whether this was prompted by the death of Katherine Armstrong two years previously is difficult to say. Her husband, Hay solicitor Herbert Rowse Armstrong, was hanged in May 1922 for her poisoning. The verdict divided the town and remains very controversial. Armstrong is the only solicitor hanged for murder in the U.K., and the case is widely viewed to have been a miscarriage of justice.[49]

There were other more mundane articles which mentioned the castle:
- A report of a local wedding listed presents including those given by Hon. Mabel Bailey, Miss Lewis, Misses Watts and Badham and Mrs Clarke, all from the castle.[50]
- In 1916 a 'beautiful Persian cat' was found at Hay Castle. Contact Hon. Gwladys Bailey.[51]

Family Wedding.

The castle was the centre of a family social event on Thurs 23 Oct 1930 when it hosted the wedding reception of the Dowager's granddaughter Marjorie Vivienne Bailey. Marjorie was born on 16 May 1910, the daughter of John Lancelot Bailey who died of influenza in India in 1918. She married Mr Oliver Powell Lancaster of Weymouth in St Mary's Church, Hay.

The bride was given away by her uncle Herbert Crawshaw Bailey, and the service was conducted by the groom's father Rev. Thomas Lancaster from St Mary's Weymouth with Rev. J.J. de Winton of Hay. The bride wore a white lace dress with an overtrain of Brussels lace loaned by her grandmother, the Dowager. The veil of white tulle fell from a wreath of orange blossom. The bouquet was of white carnations and fern, and the church was decorated with white flowers.

The bridesmaid was Miss Jacqueline Bailey the bride's sister, and best man Mr A.J. Rowbotham. The guests from outside the family included seven reverend gentlemen, three medical men and the social elite from Hay such as Major Booth, Major Cockcroft and Miss Tunnard-Moore.

The couple's honeymoon was in Lyndhurst before they sailed from London on the 'Highland Brigade' to Montevideo, Uruguay, where the groom had an appointment.[52] Oliver died in 1974 but Marjorie was still living in Uruguay in 2002, and alive on 13 January 2022 aged 111 years.

The Dowager Lady Glanusk.

The well-being of the Dowager was always newsworthy. On 5 July 1911, she was conducting a tour of the castle for choristers from Hereford Cathedral when she missed her footing at the top of a flight of steps and fell to the bottom. Fortunately, the only damage she sustained was a broken wrist and extensive bruising.

In 1913 the press reported that Lady Glanusk had returned to the castle from London following her illness.[53] Understandably there is no indication of what this might have been.

There were also regular announcements of Lady Glanusk's birthdays such as her 90th in 1930.[54] In May three years later the Brecon County Times announced that 'Dowager Lady Glanusk of Hay Castle was 93 yesterday. She is still very active for her years, gets about in her car, and only a few days ago sent out a number of invitations in her own handwriting'.[55]

Eventually, the paper had to report the sad news that on 18 April 1935 Lady Glanusk died at Hay Castle, after a seizure, just before her 95th birthday. In a short obituary, they reported she was a great philanthropist in the town and supported the House of Mercy Swansea home for unmarried mothers, as discussed earlier.

Also highlighted was her support for Hereford Eye and Ear Hospital. The original hospital was opened in leased premises on Commercial Road and provided a service to Herefordshire, neighbouring counties, and South Wales. It treated numerous miners who were prone to eye problems due to the nature of their work.

Rapidly the hospital proved to be too small for the demands made upon it. A new site was chosen in Eign Road and the foundation stone was laid on 4 December 1888 by the Countess of Chesterfield. On 20 August the next year, amid much pomp and celebration, the Victoria Eye and Ear Hospital was opened by Lady Bailey, later to become Dowager Lady Glanusk.

It was renamed the Victoria Eye Hospital in 1923 and relied heavily on voluntary donations. It transferred to the NHS in 1948 but in 2002 the service was transferred to Hereford Hospital and the building was sold. It has now been converted into apartments.

Recent archaeology has discovered an ancient key in the castle grounds.
It is heavily worn and bent but traces of gilding are still just visible.
Is this an 'original' key to the castle?

Chapter 6 – Fire! Fire!

Benjamin Guinness.

After the death of the Dowager in 1935 the castle was put up for sale for £1,500. A survey for the Council for the Protection of Rural Wales reported that it was dilapidated and in need of repairs. Historically the mix of Jacobean features, such as the fireplaces, and Georgian windows meant preservation as a historic property problematic. Institutional use as a Civic Centre was considered, or possibly the stripping of interesting features and demolition.

In the event millionaire Irish lawyer Benjamin Seymour Guinness and his son Thomas Loel Evelyn Bulkeley Guinness, the MP for Bath from 1931-45, became the tenants. Loel eventually inherited a fortune from his father, a descendant of Samuel Guinness, younger brother of Arthur Guinness founder of the famous Guinness brewery company.

Loel was the primary resident and first took out a lease in February 1936, and went on to purchase the castle for use as a fishing lodge. It came with two miles of salmon run although how often they came fishing or successful they were is unknown.

A report in the Kington Times for the week ending 22 May 1937 reported that Col. Logan of Glasbury caught seven salmon, the largest 24lbs, Mr Crawshaw on Boughrood Castle waters three, 26lbs, 20lbs and 20lbs, and Loel Guinness one, with no weight specified.

Loel and his father were not in residence when a fire broke out early on Friday 28 April 1939.[1]

Blazing Castle Drama.
In 1939 a major fire gutted the eastern portion of the mansion next to the keep. The only occupant was Mrs James the housekeeper and caretaker.
The alarm was raised by William Keylock the butcher who had a shop just below the castle. The fire broke out at 2 am and William was woken by crackling at 2.30 am. Looking out of his window he saw smoke coming from the roof so rang the telephone exchange to get them to call the police. He then sent his son Richard to the fire station, and the other two William and George to raise Mrs James. They were unable to do so and the telephone exchange had to keep ringing until Mrs James answered the phone. Six bedrooms and six bathrooms as well as valuable furniture and two staircases were destroyed. The Hereford and Brecon fire brigades were called but by the time they arrived at 4.30 am the Hay Fire Brigade under Capt. Edgar Evans had the fire under control.[2]

The butcher's shop of William Keylock before the First World War.
Photograph courtesy of Tim Pugh.

At the time it was rumoured that the fire had been caused by Mrs Kathleen James, aged 75, the housekeeper. She was the sole occupant, although she had been married in Pembroke the previous year to William Wickland.

There was a suggestion Kathleen had put clothes to air too near a fire and then left the building to visit a public house. This was questioned by one of the firemen present who knew the lady and her son Fraser. In his opinion, no 'lady' would enter a public house on her own.

The Hay Fire Brigade submitted a bill for £35.5s.0d. Their timesheet shows twelve firemen attended. The second in command William Williams was injured by a falling tile and had to leave after only one hour, but otherwise most of the others were in attendance for 12 – 16 hours although the fire was under control by about 4.30 am. For this, they were paid between £2.00 and £2.10s, at a rate of 2s.6d per hour.[3]

The fire gutted the east section of the building, destroyed the irreplaceable Jacobean staircase, and badly damaged the roof. This section of the house remained roofless and open to the elements for the next 80 years.

The eight-foot-thick west wall of this section provided an element of fire break so the spread of the fire to the rest of the mansion was largely averted, although minor damage occurred to it and a section of the roof.

On the eve of war with everyone preparing for the inevitable conflict only limited efforts could be made to repair the castle. Any remedial work would require men and materials both of which were in short supply. The site was effectively abandoned. An auction of furnishings salvaged from the fire was held on 9 May 1940 by Coggins in Cardiff.

Loel, a qualified pilot, then went off to war joining 601 the 'millionaires' Squadron R.A.F. He was Squadron Leader when they were based at R.A.F. Tangmere Sussex between December 1939 and June 1940, and fought in the Battle of Britain. Group Captain Loel Guinness survived the war.

The squadron sent detachments to Merville and Saint Valery-en-Caux in France during this time. Coincidentally Saint Valery-en-Caux was the birthplace of the most famous inhabitant of the castle - Matilda, The Lady of Hay (1155-1210).

Hay Fire Brigade

Fire at Hay Castle — Apr 28th 1939

Statement of Charges

	£	s	d
Trailer pump —			
Turn out		2	
Pumping 2 hours		8	
Officer in Charge 16 Hours	1	2	6
2nd Officer 1 do		15	
Fireman H Price 12 Hours		2	
" L Powell 12 Hours		2	
" A Price 14 Hours		2	5
" P Price 14 Hours		2	5
" A Lewis 14 Hours		2	5
" W James 14 Hours		2	5
" Eric Evans 16 Hours		2	10
" Rex Evans 16 Hours		2	10
" T Evans 6 Hours		1	5
" G Price 5 Hours		1	2

Signatures: Edgar Evans, W Williams, H Price, L Powell, P Price, A Price, A G Lewis, W James, E Evans, Rex Evans, T S Evans, G Price.

The bill from Hay Fire Brigade for attending the 1939 fire.

Victor Edward Tuson.

By the end of the war the castle site was almost derelict, and largely forgotten. In May 1946 the county council was offered the castle for £1,000 but failed to take advantage of the offer. This enabled Victor Edward Tuson of Leominster, an ex-veterinary surgeon and ex-Aston Villa footballer, to buy the unrestored castle the following year.

Victor had married into the very wealthy Studt fairground family, known throughout Wales for owning and running many of the local fairs. In September 1908, *The Cambrian* newspaper covered the wedding:

> *'Clydach, one of the most picturesque spots in the Swansea Valley, was en fete on Tuesday. Triumphal arches had been erected, flags were flying, and the merry chimes of wedding bells pealed through the place. The occasion for this excitement was the marriage of Miss Louisa Studt, eldest daughter of Mr. and Mrs. Henry Studt, Tygwyn, Clydach, to Mr. V. E. Tuson, veterinary surgeon, Marsh House, Leominster.'*

After the First World War Messrs Stutt and Tuson held a fair in Hay every spring for many years. Proceeds from one or more attractions were routinely donated to the Hay and Cusop Nursing Association or in later years Hay St John's Ambulance Brigade.

Victor went to considerable trouble to restore the damage to the main mansion, travelling far and wide to locate suitable timber. It was an enormous undertaking, but he managed to repair the roof and damaged rooms and make them waterproof and habitable again.

Attempts were made to restore the derelict east section. Some of the Dutch-style gablets were removed, numbered, and stored at ground floor level, but it was a hopeless task. It remained roofless and open to the elements for over 80 years, only held together by the encroaching ivy. Metal from redundant fairground rides, such as the dodgems, was used to blank off the empty window frames and this provided some stability to the crumbling walls.

Victor operated several amusement attractions. His main base was at Llandudno for over 30 years, but he also had sites at Aberystwyth and the Mumbles. In Hay Victor enjoyed the local fishing. His companions included Raphael Sabatini, the celebrated author of Scaramouche based at Clock Mills near Clifford, and Gerald Ralph Desmond Browne the flamboyant 7th Lord Kenmore. Gerald was a famous journalist and gossip writer, writing 'Londoners Log' in the Sunday Express.

It is said that many offers from Americans were made to buy the castle,[4] possibly destined to be dismantled and shipped across to America. Who knows? Was this just another Hay tall story?

Victor died in January 1964 aged 77, leaving an estate valued at £66,000, and is buried in the family vault at Leominster. His executors put the castle up for sale.

Richard Booth - Coeur de Libre.

By 1962 Hay was in the process of winding down. Like many small rural towns, it was unable to compete with new shopping trends and competition from supermarkets. Shop after shop was closing. The town was dying.

It was at this time that Richard George William Pitt Booth (12.09.1938-20.08.2019) opened his first bookshop. Richard was born in Plymouth to Philip Booth an army officer. After schooling at Rugby, he went to Oxford University to read history.

In 1960 while he was still at Oxford Kathleen, the widow of Richard's uncle Major William Henry Booth DSO, OBE, died. Their six-bedroomed house Brynmelin in Cusop then appeared briefly on the housing market.

Advertisement for Brynmelin in 1960.

Regardless of the circumstances, Richard's parents moved into Brynmelin. Richard always maintained that his father inherited it, and in due course it became Richard's home.

When Richard came down from Oxford his father was keen that Richard acquire a profession and arranged for him to work at an accountancy firm in the city. Richard said he walked out after two weeks.

The old fire station at the top of Castle Street was vacant and Richard acquired it, opening an antique and second-hand bookshop. Rapidly this became first and foremost a bookshop. People scoffed 'No one reads books in Hay', but somebody did. Within a few years he created a bookselling empire, having books in some 27 properties across the town.

He was very generous, supporting and encouraging any of his staff who felt inclined to open their own bookshops. By the 1970s Hay was becoming the 'Town of Books'.

Hay Castle Bookshop.

It was around the time he bought his bookshop that Hay Castle came up for sale. After a potential purchaser considering it as an antique centre pulled out, Richard was able to buy it from Victor Tuson's estate for £5,000. Clearing out all the old fairground paraphernalia Richard turned the ground floor into a bookshop.

The first floor became the centre of his business operations, accommodation was available for visiting book dealers, and riotous parties were held. As the years went by books began to fill every nook and cranny of every floor of the mansion.

Richard entered the book trade at an auspicious time. American universities were expanding their libraries. At the same time, English stately homes and fine mansions were experiencing severe financial difficulties. This led them to sell their libraries. For an astute businessman, this was a fertile hunting ground and Richard was that businessman. He said that within five years his business turnover increased from £6,000 to over £100,000, and 10 years later he was a millionaire.

The reduction in workforce and closure of coal mines from 1960 to 1985 meant the dismantling of mining institutes and clubs. These held innumerable weighty, learned, and often rare books, donated by benefactors for the 'edification of the working man'.

Richard was able to purchase books worth many thousands of pounds at knockdown prices. Many of his buying trips were to America where he claimed he bought a greater volume of second-hand books than anyone else. He made five book-buying visits to America in the first four months of 1979 alone.

Richard claimed that a library of 12,000 dictionaries, all different, went to him, as did 14,000 books from a Danish castle. These were then bought by the University of Toronto for $100,000.

Adverts regularly appeared in the Illustrated London News and Birmingham Daily Post throughout the late 1960s and 1970s offering to buy books. Regular free book-buying coach trips were laid on from Birmingham to Hay.

A typical advertisement appeared in the Aberdeen Evening Express:

'Books Bought.
Any quantities from a single volume to a complete library purchased.
Offers made without obligation.
Please write to Richard Booth Booksellers Ltd. Hay Castle Hay on Wye.'

Richard Booth – Coeur de Libre.
Plaque sculptured by Penny Chantler.

Richard led a tumultuous life and the castle became his 'guest accommodation' away from Brynmelin. Here he entertained everyone from pop stars to visiting luminaries, and always a variety of book dealers.

The castle provided the setting for a musical weekend in September 1975. The Opera Buffa Society, which specialised in comic opera, performed Pergolesi's La Serva Padrona in aid of the National Society for Mentally Handicapped Children. The Stage hoped it would become an annual event but like so many of Richard's schemes this failed to fully materialise.[5]

Richard married three times. By his own admission, he maintained that his wives had a lot to put up with 'marrying a kind of monster'. The eccentric visitors Richard invited to the castle did not help, although eventually he found his life partner.

After he first married, he wrote a book 'A Varsity Lad and a Lass' under the pen name Gwalio'r Gwynn (1970).[6] The book was a typical Richard gesture. His choice of pen name had no connection with the book 'The Land of Regrets' by Isobel Fraser Hunter which is set in Gwalior, an important state near Agra in India.

Independence of Hay.

The castle was also the setting for his outrageous stunts. The one that gained the most publicity, and put Hay on the map, was on 1 April 1977. Richard declared himself 'King of Hay', Coeur de Livre, and the Independence of Hay on Wye from the European Economic Community, predecessor to the Common Market, and subsequently the European Union. (Brexit happened in Hay first!).

On the lawns in the front of the castle, Richard was resplendent in his royal regalia. This consisted of a crown decorated with cotton wool balls, an orb made from a copper ballcock and a sceptre from a copper plumbing pipe with brass fittings. Richard's prime minister was his horse Goldie, his navy was a raft on the river Wye, and a two-seater Tiger Moth was Richard's air force.

April Ashley, who claimed to be the ninth person in the world to undergo gender reassignment surgery in 1960, and the first in the United Kingdom, was the Duchess of Hay and Offa's Dyke. After surgery April had a tumultuous life. She became a model and entered high society in London, but life was fraught for her once her background became general knowledge. Escaping to Hay, April settled there for a time, finding a welcome among the eccentric circle of personalities that built up around Richard. April left to live in California and died in December 2021 aged 86 years.

Richard's well-publicised coronation stunt attracted the attention of several television crews and made headlines around the world. It effectively put Hay, and its castle, on the 20th-century map.

The Fire.

Later that year on 30 November a major fire destroyed the habitable part of the castle used by Richard, causing damage estimated to be over £100,000. Fortunately Richard and his housekeeper escaped unharmed.

The upper floor of the mansion after the 1977 fire.
Photograph courtesy of Hay Castle Trust.

The part-time firemen from Hay battled for four hours to bring the fire under control. Despite rumours to the contrary arson was ruled out.[7] Richard always maintained that the fire was caused by a log rolling out of a first-floor fireplace after he had gone to bed.

This time the remaining undamaged part of the castle was destroyed. Items lost included the panelled rooms, the Georgian staircase in the front hall, and many roof timbers.

The main restoration work was started by Capps and Capps of Hereford. One of their key headaches was finding new beams for the roof and floors. For these they required oak tree trucks free of any branches for the first thirty feet.

In 2017 a farmer rang the Hay Castle Trust to enquire if he could 'come and see his tree'. He supplied one of the beams during this restoration.

In the great storm of 1987, a large oak had fallen in his garden. He received a telephone call and was able to confirm that his oak was the necessary 30-foot length. A couple of days later a lorry arrived with workmen who proceeded to cut the tree up, pay him £150 and remove the trunk they wanted.

This beam is easy to identify as it is one of the few 'complete' original beams that originally supported the roof and attics. Most of the others are composed of sections of old beams spliced together. Fortunately, they do not have to take a great deal of weight now as in the redevelopment new roof timbers were installed to strengthen and support the roof.

One of the first-floor fireplaces required a new lintel. Richard mentioned this in his local 'watering hole' the Masons Arms (now the Spa supermarket) one evening and the landlord Ken Jenkins offered to lend him a stone of the necessary dimensions.

This stone is something of an enigma. It is covered in crude figurative and decorative carvings. Legend has it that it was a medieval field boundary, but the obviously male figure suggests a fertility symbol. Alfred Watkins, the famous Herefordshire archaeologist, antiquarian and developer of the theory of 'ley lines', had photographed it many years previously outside Francis Kilverts vicarage in Clyro.

How it ended up in the Masons Arms in Castle Street is unknown. The stone formed a useful lintel until the recent redevelopment when it was removed and returned to the owner's family.

Part of the puzzling lintel in the first-floor fireplace.

By 2002 Richard's restoration work was almost complete and on 4 April the castle was the venue to celebrate the 25th anniversary of Independence. The sweeping room occupying the whole width of the first floor was the setting for a 'State Banquet'. Here Richard was declared 'Emperor of all the World's Second-hand Book Towns'.

After suitable refreshments, the party then proceeded outside into a storm-lashed evening for Richard to give an impassioned speech from a wooden platform overlooking the market square. He said that he felt this was the first, and possibly only, time he was appreciated by the locals. They were looking for leadership against local property development.

Independent of the work restoring the mansion the Welsh Government historic buildings organisation CADW undertook emergency work on the castle keep during the 1970s. Steel beans were inserted into the fireplaces built into the north wall in the 1570s. These provided additional support to the original wooden lintels. The tops of the walls of the keep were also capped with mortar to stabilize them.

Honesty Bookshop.

Richard always maintained that the biggest hazard of the second-hand book trade is that 90% of the books are unsellable. Only a fraction of a percentage of any collection are of real value. How to dispose of these unsellable books was a constant problem.

One solution was the council refuse dump at Clyro. This reputedly had the most intellectual bonfire in the country. Richard caused outrage when he started offering a full car boot of books as fuel for the fire at five shillings a load – free to Old Age Pensioners.

As part of his efforts to get rid of them, he had open shelves put all around the lawn at the base of the front terraces of the castle. In the middle was a trailer. Shelves and trailer were filled to overflowing with books. All of these were available for a nominal sum on an honesty box basis. Richard claimed his greatest achievement was the creation of the concept of Honesty Bookshops, and his legacy to the art of bookselling is still maintained on this lawn today.

Merchandise.

Ever looking for money-making opportunities, and publicity for the town, Richard offered Titles of Peerage to 'loyal supporters of the kingdom'. He offered to confer the title of duke, earl, baron, lord or knight, with appropriate titles for their partners, to anyone with a sufficient claim. These were confirmed by the passing of a sum of money!

He also issued passports, Hay car stickers, various publications and a 45rpm record 'The King of Hay's Greatest Hits'. This included the Hay National Anthem. It failed to make the best-seller singles chart.

Finale.

Over the years many were the escapades associated with this flamboyant eccentric who had an aversion to autocratic local government interference. As king, he claimed to defend the rights of his 1500 subjects against bureaucracy, as well as exploit any business opportunity.[8]

Examples of this are the booklets he published - such as 'Abolish the Wales Tourist Board', 'God Save Us from the Development Board of Rural Wales', 'Bureaucracy in Brecon and Radnor with reference to a horse ride through Cusop Dingle' (which is in England), and 'Bring Back Horses'.

Another example of his outgoing personality was the occasion when Richard asked the stewardess on a flight to America to announce that 'The King of Hay is on board'. At this, all the passengers erupted into rousing applause.

Richard had many varied and madcap aspirations. He declared from the castle ramparts that he would create a thriving export market for his Hay Sausage. An accompanying photograph showed Nigel Keylock, from the butchers shop just below the castle, with hands full of strings of sausages. Nigel was one of the sons of William Keylock who raised the alert about the castle fire in 1939.

Current opinion is that the sausage recipe was developed by Bill Powell, a butcher further down Castle Street with a shop opposite Richards Honesty Bookshop. Such technicalities did not deter Richard's escapades.

Richard's parties were renowned for including pop stars and personalities, as detailed in his autobiography.[9] He claimed that pop star Marianne Faithful and the model April Ashley were regular attendees.

On one occasion two partygoers climbed the steps above the great gates onto the castle walls. Somehow, whether it was under the influence of the party, the view, or the company we will never know, one of them managed to fall into the portcullis slot.

Fortunately, the person concerned was of 'ample proportions' so he stuck near the top of the opening. After an hour's deliberations the fire brigade managed to winch him out to safety.

Richard was made an M.B.E in 2004 for services to Welsh Tourism. He retained the castle until 2011 when he sold it to the Hay Castle Trust. He died on 20 August 2019 aged 80 years.

For more on a true eccentric see https://www.walesartsreiew.org/richard-booth-king-of-hay/.

Chapter 7 - Hay Castle Trust.

The Hay Castle Trust was founded in 2011 and acquired the castle for a reputed £2M. Once the trust was established planning for a comprehensive restoration started in earnest. As a Grade I Scheduled monument this was a mammoth undertaking and required substantial funding.

An initial application was made to the National Lottery Heritage Fund. This indicated support in principle and released 'pump priming' money to work up a full formal application. This required multiple submissions such as the historical context of the building, plans, costings, surveys of the environment, bats, other wildlife, support from heritage organisations etc. Community involvement had to be demonstrated, as well as continuing commercial solvency.

An archaeological investigation was necessary. None had ever been undertaken on the site while it was under private ownership and test pits were dug in 2018. Mostly these revealed little of historic interest although clarification of the configuration of the gates in the keep tower was obtained, and a solitary trebuchet ball was discovered. This has been dated to 1265 and the time of Simon de Montfort's rebellion. How it ended up at the castle is a mystery.

Excavation of the front lawn was a challenge. After removal of the turf, first trowels, then spades and finally a JCB excavator had to be used to find the medieval surface. As previously discussed this demonstrated that the front lawn is covered with two metres of topsoil. This must have been deposited all over the site before the building of the main Jacobean mansion in the 1630s.

Little of archaeological significance was found beyond the fragments of glass, a key, a civil war musket powder measure and a trade token of Matthew Parry who died *c.*1690. Eventually the trust obtained National Lottery grant funding of £4.45M.

While this was going on the Trust worked to raise the additional match funding of £1.6M, a condition of the National Lottery grant. As a Schedule I building all redevelopment plans had to be agreed upon by multiple heritage bodies, the Brecon Beacons National Park, etc. Once this was obtained redevelopment could commence. Work started in 2018 and then eight months later the pandemic struck and disrupted work for the next two years. The redevelopment was finally completed at the start of the 2022 Hay International Literary Festival, the week before the Spring Bank Holiday.

The renovation work has been extensive, and to a very high standard according to heritage experts. The derelict section, open to the elements since the 1939 fire, has a new roof, and two mezzanine floors have been inserted. These now link the main mansion to the keep and allow access to a viewing platform giving extensive views across the Radnorshire hills. The repair work done after the 1977 fire has been reviewed and redone where necessary to bring it up to current best heritage standards.

The castle gates dating from 1340 and 1640 have been repaired, strengthened by hidden stainless steel rods, and rehung. It is believed they are the oldest 'in situ' gates in the country. Behind them, the opening that contained the beam used to slide across and bar the gates still contains a wooden lining. This has been dated to 980 i.e. it was recycled when the gateway was built.

While the preparatory work was being undertaken the trust forged links with the summer and winter Hay International Literary Festivals. The first Hay Festival was in 1988 and Richard Booth was strongly opposed to it. He suspected that it would generate money for its London backers and that Hay would not see any benefit. As a consequence, it received no support from him or use of the castle for events. His supposition was not entirely wrong, but in general the community has benefitted to some extent.

The trust worked to establish links with the festival. While waiting for funding for the restoration, and the necessary planning permissions, a small number of events were hosted within the castle precincts. The day the castle reopened its gates to the public a festival event, an open-air rendition of Shakespeare's Julius Caesar, was enacted on the front lawn.

On the 7 July 2022 H.R.H. The Prince of Wales officially opened the restored castle, after four years of work and a £6,000,000 investment. The castle is now open seven days a week throughout the year.

Future activities at the castle will revolve around exhibitions, functions, presentations, concerts, workshops, and other educational activities. There is a café serving hot food all day, and in the evenings when events are taking place. Inevitably there is a bookshop; after all, this is Hay 'Town of Books'.

It is possible to hire the castle as a wedding and events venue, the first floor is configured as an education space with a printing press, and on the second floor there is an exhibition space of national standard. The lawns have become a 'village green' hosting multiple events and community activities.

After being largely derelict for nearly a century the castle has been rejuvenated, with an exciting future to look forward to.

References

Bradley, Bramwell, *Within The Castle Walls*, private printing (N.D.).
Evans, Christopher J., Guillimard F.H.H. ed. *Breconshire,* Cambridge County Geographies (1912).
Fairs, Geoffrey L., *A History Of The Hay*, Phillimore, Chichester, (1972).
Fairs, Geoffrey L., *Annals of a Parish,* Phillimore, Chichester, (1994).
Holden, Brock W., King John, the Braoses and the Celtic Fringe 1207-1216, *Albion: Journal of British Studies* v.33 (2001).
Ivinson, Stuart, *Anglo-Welsh Wars 1050-1300*, Bridge Books (2001).
Jones, Theophilus, *The History of Brecknockshire.* Blissett, Davies and Sons, Brecon (1909,1911) Brecknock Society (1930).
Jones, Thomas, ed., *Brut y Tywysogyon (The Chronicle of the Princes), Peniarth MS. 20 version,* University of Wales Press (1952).
King, D. J. Cathcart, *The Castle in England and Wales: An Interpretative History,* London, Routledge (1991).
Nicholls, Alan James, *Historical Directory of Hay on Wye*, Lulu (2014).
Nicholls, Alan James, *Lords of the Manor,* Lulu (2016).
Plomer, William, *Kilvert's Diaries,* Jonathan Cape (1977).
Remfry, Paul M., *Hay on Wye Castle 1066 to 1298,* SCS Publishing (1995).
Remfry, Paul M. *Castles of Breconshire,* Logaston Press (1999).
Renton, Charles, *The Story of Herefordshire's Hospitals*, Logaston Press (1999).
Smith, Lucy Toulmin, *The Itinerary in Wales of John Leland in or about the years 1536-1539,* Geo Bell and Sons, London (1906).
https://archive.org/details/itineraryinwales00lelauoft/page/n7/mode/2up.
Soldat, Rob, *A Walk around Hay*, RL Marches Vade Mecum (2007).
Spencer, Dan, *The Castle at War in Medieval England and Wales*, Amberley (2018).
Suggettt, Richard, *Hay Castle and Haysland: The Architectural Personality of a Marcher Lordship,* Brycheiniog vol. LII (2021) 23-57.

BCT – Brecon County Times.
NLW – National Library of Wales.

Notes.
_____

Chapter 1.

[1] Evans, Christopher J., Guillimard F.H.H. ed. *Breconshire*, Cambridge County Geographies (1912)

[2] Ford, Peter, *Weston. The Often Forgotten Suburb of Hay on Wye*, Amazon (2022).

[1] Ford, Peter, *Matilda - The Lady of Hay*, Logastone Press (2021).

[2] Jones, Thomas, ed., *Brut y Tywysogyon (The Chronicle of the Princes), Peniarth MS. 20 version* U. of Wales Press (1952).

[3] R.W.B., Early History of Hay and its Lordship. *Archaeologia Cambrensis* vol.XIV no. LV (July 1883).

[4] Walker, David, *Medieval Wales*, Cambridge University Press (1990) 53.

[5] Fairs, Geoffrey, *The History of the Hay*, Phillimore (1972).

[6] Smith, Lucy Toulmin, *The Itinerary in Wales of John Leland in or about the years 1536-1539*, G. Bell and Sons (1906).

Chapter 2.

[9] *Hay Castle Glass*, a report commissioned for Hay Castle Trust by Hay History Group.

[10] Fairs, Geoffrey, *The History of the Hay*, Phillimore (1972).

[11] Stirnet.com https://www.stirnet.com/genie/data/british/gg/gwynne1.php#lnk1.

[12] *High Sheriff of Brecknockshire,* retrieved 18 December 2021. https://www.wikiwand.com/en/High_Sheriff_of_Brecknockshire.

[13] *Cardiff and Merthyr Guardian* (23.10.1863).

[14] Soldat, Rob, *A Walk around Hay,* RL Marches Vade Mecum (2007).

[15] National Archives London, *Star ch.8/154/3*.

[16] *Hay Castle, British Listed Buildings,* https://britishlistedbuildings.co.uk/300007405-hay-castle-hay#.Yb8rTS-l1KO.

[17] Dinley Thomas, *The Account of the official progress of His Grace Henry the first Duke of Beaufort... through Wales in 1684 : by photo-lithography from the original MS of Thomas Dineley ... / preface by Richard W. Banks* (1888). Royal Collection Trust.

[18] *Hay Castle Glass,* a report commissioned for Hay Castle Trust by Hay History Group.

[19] North Wales Chronicle, *Cambrian Guide,* (11.11.1865), 611.

[20] Ford, Peter, *Doctors, Disease, and Death. The Story of Public Health in Hay on Wye*, Amazon (2021).

[21] Drawn by Robert Batty, d.. 1848. Engraved by Edward Francis Finde, 1791-1857. This image is available from the National Library of Wales and can be viewed in its original context on the NLW Catalogue, CC0, https://commons.wikimedia.org/w/index.php?curid=48260108.

[22] Nicholls, Alan, *The Lords of Hay*, Lulu (2016).

[23] *NLW,* ref. 274.

[24] *NLW*. DD 157.

[25] *Hereford Journal* (12.02.1874).

[26] Ford, Peter, *Mary Morgan Victim or Villain of Infanticide*. Amazon (2020).

[27] *Hereford Journal* 20.01.1791).

[28] *Hereford Journal* (25.11.1795).

[29] *Hereford Journal* (28.06.1809).

[30] *NLW,* ref.4065-6 (1813).

[31] *Hereford Journal* (19.03.1806).

[32] *Cambrian* (08.09.1821).

[33] *Hereford Journal* (29.08.1821).

[34] *Hereford Journal* (23.06.1826).

[35] *Brecon County Times* (15.04.1876).

[36] *Westmorland Gazette* (10.04.1819).

Chapter 3.
[1] *Hereford Journal* (10.11.1826).
[2] *Cambrian* (17.04.1824).
[3] *Hereford Journal* (16.04.1828).
[4] *Clifton Society* (19.09.1901).
[5] *Hampshire Telegraph* (03.09.1915).
[6] https://ghgraham.org/walterdewinton1781.html.
[7] *Hereford Journal* (06.03.1839).
[8] *Hereford Journal* (26.07.1843).
[9] *Hereford Journal* (02.08.1843).
[10] *Hereford Journal* (09.08.1843).
[11] *Hereford Journal* (17.01.1844).
[12] *Cambrian* (September 1826).
[13] *Cambrian* (05.05.1827).
[14] *Cambrian* (23.04.1828).
[15] *Hereford Journal* (20.05.1829).
[16] Fairs, Geoffrey, *The History of the Hay*, Phillimore (1972).
[17] *Monmouth Merlin* (26.10.1844).
[18] *CADW Full Report of Listed Buildings* https://cadwpublic-api.azurewebsites.net/reports/listedbuilding/FullReport?lang=en&id=7341.
[19] This image of the keep by John George Wood 1816 is available from the National Library of Wales and can be viewed in its original context on the NLW Catalogue, CC0, https://commons.wikimedia.org/w/index.php?curid=48260108.
[20] Jones, Peter, *On the Eve of the Great War: some aspects of the clergy of Breconshire at the census of 1911*, Brycheiniog vol.LII (2021)58-71.
[21] Scott, Christina, *A Historian and His World: A life of Christopher Dawson,* Transaction Publishers (1992).
[22] *Cambrian* (19.07.1849).
[23] *Weston Super Mare Gazette* (14.01.1891).
[24] Scott, Christina, *A Historian and His World: The Life of Christopher Dawson*, Transaction Publishers (1984).
[25] Philip Dawson in the W.R. Mitchel Archives https://www.wrmitchellarchive.org.uk/node/73.
[26] Scott, Christina, *A Historian and his World. A Life of Christopher Dawson*, Transaction Publishers (1984).
[27] Morgan, W.E.T, *Hay and Neighbourhood,* H.R. Grant (*c.*1930).
[28] *BCT* (28.08.1885).
[29] *St James Gazette* (5.10.1886).
[30] Plomer, William, *Kilvert's Diaries,* Jonathan Cape (1977).
[1] Barnwell, E.L., Relic of Ann Boleyn, *Archaeologia Cambrensis* Third Series no. 37 (January 1864) 133-4.
[2] Fforde, Mari, Ann Boleyn's Brooch and the Bevans in *Hay on Wye History Notes* (2018).

Chapter 4.
[3] *BCT* (03.02.1905).
[4] *BCT* (24.08.1906).
[5] *BCT* (09.08.1917).
[6] *BCT* (06.09.1923).
[7] *BCT* (06.08.1931).
[8] *Western Mail* (14.05.1929).

[9] *Country Life* (1916).
[10] *BCT* (23.10.1913).
[11] *BCT* (14.05.1931).
[12] *BCT* (23.01.1913).
[13] Anand, Anita *Sophia: Princess, Suffragette, Revolutionary*. Bloomsbury (2015).
[14] *BCT* (5.02.1925).
[15] *Western Mail* (27.03.1914).
[16] *BCT* (23.04.1914).
[17] *BCT* (03.07.1919).
[18] *BCT* (24.06.1920).
[19] *BCT* (15.11.1923).
[20] *BCT* (02.10.1924).
[21] *BCT* (06.11.1924).
[22] *BCT* (09.07.1925).
[23] *Northampton Mercury* (05.12.1924).
[24] *BCT* (26.09.1926).
[25] *Weston Mail* (17.09.1930).
[26] *BCT* (02 .04.931).
[27] *BCT* (03.06.1931).
[28] *BCT* (07.09.1933).
[29] *BCT* (19.10.1933).
[30] *BCT* (19.11.1914).
[31] *BCT* (28.12.1916).
[32] *BCT* (31.10.1918).
[33] *BCT* (24.02.1916).
[34] *BCT* (20.03.1919).
[35] Bradley, Bramwell, *Within The Castle Walls In Service 1928*, reprint by Reprintuk, Loughborough (nd).
[36] *BCT* (1928).
[37] Hay Millennium Society, *Nobody Had Heard of Hay,* Logaston Press (2002).

Chapter 5.
[1] *BCT* (27.08.1914).
[2] *BCT* (13.08.1914).
[3] *BCT* (19.11.1914).
[4] *BCT* (13.07.1916).
[5] *BCT* (14.06.1916).
[6] *BCT* (28.01.1915).
[7] *BCT* (26.08.1915).
[8] *BCT* (09.12.1915).
[9] *Brecon and Radnor Express* (2.12.1915).
[10] *BCT* (13.02.1913).
[11] *BCT* (14.05.1914).
[12] *BCT* (29.04.1915).
[13] *BCT* (13.01.1916).
[14] *Western Mail* (03.04.1918).

[15] *BCT* (21.07.1921).
[16] *BCT* (13.01.1916).
[17] *BCT* (28.02.1918).
[18] *BCT* (03.04.1919).
[19] Europeans in East Africa.
https://www.europeansineastafrica.co.uk/ site/custom/database/?a=viewIndividual&pid=2&person=21242.
Downloaded 10 May 2022.
[20] *BCT* (08.08.1916).
[21] *Pontypool Free Press* (5.04.1907).
[22] *BCT* (02.09.1913).
[23] *BCT* (04.06.1914).
[24] *BCT* (09.07.1914).
[25] *BCT* (26.07.1917).
[26] *BCT* (29.05.1919).
[27] *BCT* (14.08.1919).
[28] BCT (17.06.1926).
[29] *Western Mail* (12.10.1928).
[30] *BCT* (18.07.1912).
[31] *BCT* (14.12.1922).
[32] *BCT* (03.05.1925).
[33] *BCT* (03.12.1925).
[34] *Merthyr Express* (26.10.1933).
[35] *Weston Mail* (18.10.1934).
[36] *BCT* (27.07.1933).
[37] *BCT* (03.01.1924).
[38] *BCT* (09.09.1926).
[39] *BCT* (12.05.1932)
[40] Ford, Peter, *Matilda Lady of Hay*, Logaston (2021).
[41] *BCT* (11.02.1911).
[42] McLeod, Kembrew, *The Fake 'Asian' Who Fooled 18th-Century London* www.theatlantic.com downloaded 30 April 2022.
[43] George Psalmanazar, *Memoirs*, London (1764).
[44] *Radnor Express* (28.02.1907).
[45] *BCT* (04.02.1915).
[46] *BCT* (17.12.1914).
[47] *BCT* (16.12.1915).
[48] *BCT* (15.09.1923).
[49] Beales, Martin, *The Hay Poisoner,* Robert Hale (1997).
[50] *BCT* (04.02.1915).
[51] *BCT* (20.11.1916).
[52] *Western Mail* (24.10.1924).
[53] *BCT* (04.12.1913).
[54] *Kington Times* (10.05.1930).
[55] *BCT* (04.05.1933.

Chapter 6.
[1] *Bath Weekly Chronicle and Herald* (29.04.1939).
[2] *Western Mail* (29.04.1939).
[3] *Haywire 66* (June 1965).
[4] *North Wales Weekly News* (16.07.1964).
[5] *The Stage* (25.08.1975).
[6] Gwynn, Gwalio'r, *A Varsity Lad and a Lass*, NLW MS 20623D (1970).
[7] *Birmingham Daily Post* (30.11.1977).
[8] *Illustrated London News* (01.07.1981).
[9] Booth, Richard, *My Kingdom of Books*, Y Lolfa (1999).

Milton Keynes UK
Ingram Content Group UK Ltd.
UKHW050414050424
440544UK00002B/18